D1212850

ANCIENT AMERICAN POTTERY

The Faber Monographs on Pottery and Porcelain
Edited by W. B. Honey and Arthur Lane

*

German Porcelain *by* W. B. Honey
Early Islamic Pottery *by* Arthur Lane
English Delftware *by* F. H. Garner
Corean Pottery *by* W. B. Honey
French Faïence *by* Arthur Lane
Medieval English Pottery *by* Bernard Rackham
Wedgwood Ware *by* W. B. Honey
Greek Pottery *by* Arthur Lane
French Porcelain of the Eighteenth Century *by* W. B. Honey
Later Chinese Porcelain *by* Soame Jenyns
Early Staffordshire Pottery *by* Bernard Rackham
Nineteenth-Century English Pottery and Porcelain *by* Geoffrey Bemrose
English Porcelain of the Eighteenth Century *by* J. L. Dixon
Italian Maiolica *by* Bernard Rackham
Early Chinese Pottery and Porcelain *by* Basil Gray
Worcester Porcelain *by* F. A. Barrett
Ming Pottery and Porcelain *by* Soame Jenyns
Italian Porcelain *by* Arthur Lane
Oriental Blue-and-White *by* Sir Harry Garner
Artist Potters in England *by* Muriel Rose
Roman Pottery *by* R. J. Charleston
Ancient American Pottery *by* G. H. S. Bushnell and Adrian Digby

in preparation

Bow Porcelain *by* J. L. Dixon
Later Islamic Pottery: Persia, Syria and Turkey *by* Arthur Lane
Hispano-Moresque Ware *by* Arthur Lane
Chelsea Porcelain *by* J. L. Dixon
Scandinavian Pottery and Porcelain *by* R. J. Charleston
Japanese Porcelain *by* Soame Jenyns
Japanese Pottery *by* Soame Jenyns
Frankenthal Pottery *by* R. J. Charleston
Longton Hall Porcelain *by* Bernard Watney
English Cream Coloured Wares *by* Donald Towner

A. *Portrait vase, Mochica culture, Peru, probably 7th century* A.D.
Height $12\frac{5}{8}$ *in. British Museum*
(*See p.* 32)

ANCIENT AMERICAN POTTERY

by

G. H. S. BUSHNELL

and

ADRIAN DIGBY

FABER AND FABER
24 Russell Square
London

First published in mcmlv
by Faber and Faber Limited
24 *Russell Square London W.C.*1
Printed in Great Britain by
R. MacLehose and Company Limited
The University Press Glasgow
Blocks made and colour plates printed by
Fine Art Engravers Limited
London, Esher and Guildford

FOREWORD

The authors are jointly responsible for the introduction. Mr. Digby has written the chapters on Central America, and Dr. Bushnell has written those on the Southwest of the United States and South America, but each has agreed to the conclusions of the other. They are fully aware that there are differences in the detailed treatment of their respective chapters, but these are partly due to variations in the data available, and some are, in any case, inevitable in cooperation of this sort. Most of the material illustrated comes from the British Museum and the Cambridge University Museum of Archaeology and Ethnology, but the authors are very grateful to the following for photographs and permission to publish them:

Denver Museum of Natural History, Col., U.S.A., and Dr. H. M. Wormington, Curator of Archaeology in the Museum, for Plate 4B.

Arizona State Museum, U.S.A., and Dr. Emil W. Haury, Director, for Plate 9.

Señor Fernando Gamboa, Commissioner General of the Mexican Art Exhibition, London 1953 and Dr. Luis Aveleyra, for permission to photograph and reproduce specimens shown in that Exhibition, whether belonging to Official Institutions or to private collectors. (Plates 12, 13, 16, 22, 23, 26, 31 and 36A.) Individual owners will be found under the description for each plate.

Etnografiska Museet, Göteborg, Sweden and Dr. K. G. Izikowitz, Director, for Plates 54, 55.

CONTENTS

ILLUSTRATIONS

COLOUR PLATES

MONOCHROME PLATES

at the end of the book

PLATES

MAPS

TABLE

1

INTRODUCTION

For many years, one of the deepest and most disputed problems in human history has been whether or not the higher civilizations of the New World developed in isolation from those of the Old. Whatever standpoint we adopt over this question, whether we believe in cultural influence from the Old World or whether we believe that American civilizations evolved without influence from outside, there is throughout all American art a feeling or treatment that strikes us as characteristically American.

This is not to say that all American art is homogeneous—for in no continent is there greater artistic diversity—but there is a quality about all American art which enables us, even if we do not recognize the exact provenance of an object, to say that it is of aboriginal American workmanship. This underlying feeling, produced perhaps by different senses of values from those of the Old World, is nowhere more noticeable than in the pottery. The study of the pottery of Mexico and Peru and of the neighbouring countries generally lends support to the view that America owes little to the Old World, though occasional examples bear a striking, but probably superficial, resemblance to certain oriental shapes and decorative motifs.

Much American pottery is of surprising excellence both in fabric and in design, but many features of Old World ceramics are lacking. Porcelain is unknown, glaze is rarely used as an ornament and never as a waterproofing agent, and the potters were ignorant of the wheel. The commonest technique was the primitive one of building up from coils or rings of clay, hand modelling was often employed, and casting from moulds was widespread and was in use by the early part of the first millennium B.C. The complete absence of the wheel is of fundamental importance to any study of American pottery, for, revolving at high speed and imparting a centrifugal force to the clay under the potter's hand, it imposes a symmetry on the vessel and allows the possibility of almost infinite variety. If, on the other hand, one of the more primitive processes is employed, there is a far greater restriction to more or less traditional forms. American pottery, therefore, lacks something of the technical perfection of much Old World pottery, but it gains in charm from the subtle variations imposed by hand working.

The use of the oxidizing flame for firing red, brown and orange wares, and of the reducing flame for firing black and grey ones, was mastered at an early date. Slips and paints of many colours were used in finishing the pots, and freehand designs, some of them of great intricacy, were painted on them. The surfaces were in many cases highly burnished with a pebble or some similar object. Tempering material varied from place to place. Sand, calcite or crushed potsherds were all used on occasion, and in some cases, where the unbaked clay was not sufficiently ductile, powdered mica was added. This gave the pots a curious glistening appearance, which has given rise to the unfounded belief that gold dust was added to the clay. In common with weaving and other crafts, New World pottery demonstrates the possession of great manual skill with very simple apparatus.

Judging by experience in other parts of the world where the wheel is not used, and by modern practice among American Indians, pottery was normally, but not necessarily always, a woman's craft. The sight of a Pueblo Indian woman, in a village in Arizona or New Mexico, squatting on the ground and building up a pot with deft fingers from a long roll of clay, or painting it with sure strokes of the brush, is a vivid reminder of countless generations who have made their pots in the same way, not only on the arid plateaux of the south-western United States, but also in the tropical forests of Central America, the bleak highlands of the Andes and the desert coast of Peru.

The first known appearances of pottery in America are in the second millennium B.C., and our survey will with one exception end with the coming of the Europeans early in the sixteenth century. The area from which our examples are taken stretches in latitude from the southern United States to northern Chile, and within this will be found numerous highly characteristic local styles, some of which gave place to new ones after a comparatively short life. The highest of the New World civilizations are found in Mexico and the countries on its southern border, and in Peru, and these must occupy much of our space, but notable examples come from other regions, particularly the Southwest of the United States, Panamá, Nicaragua and Costa Rica. The subject will be treated by areas beginning in the north and working southward through Mexico and the Central American States to South America. It will be necessary to omit many areas, including Eastern South America and the West Indies, and only the better-known wares will be considered, for a short work of this nature is no place for a detailed analysis of the myriad obscure pottery styles of America.

2

THE SOUTHWEST OF THE U.S.A.

The best ancient pottery in the United States comes from the south-west, where the descendants of the old potters still work in the traditional way. The south-west comprises the States of Arizona and New Mexico, it extends into the south of Utah and Colorado, and part of North Mexico belongs to the same archaeological province. It is an arid land where rainfall is sparse, but it includes irrigable valleys and there are favoured places on the uplands where maize and other crops can be grown. It has been inhabited from early times by peaceful agricultural peoples, who have had to work hard to wrest a living from the soil. Its great sweeps of desert, its wide horizons and its clear skies exercise a peculiar fascination over those who know it, and visitors generally seek opportunity to return there.

It was formerly inhabited by three main groups of people, each with its characteristic pottery types. The plateau which occupies the north and middle of the region was the home of the Anasazi, whose descendants, the Pueblo Indians, are still found there. The desert valleys of the Gila and Salt rivers, which lie south and west of the plateau, were the seat of the Hohokam. In south-western New Mexico in a hilly region where the Mimbres valley runs down towards the Mexican border, was a third people to whose culture the name of Mogollon has been given, but their pottery styles are not so well known as those of the other two, with two notable exceptions which will be mentioned in their place.

The Anasazi

Early representatives of the Anasazi were living in the south-west at the beginning of the Christian era, but they made no pottery and are named Basketmakers after their fine baskets, most of which were made by the coiling method. They eventually began to mould vessels of clay mixed with vegetable fibres in baskets and dry them in the sun. Some of these were accidentally burnt, and this may have given rise to the idea of pottery among them, but it may have been introduced from elsewhere, since they were by no means the first people in America to make it. Until about A.D. 500, evidence for house building is scarce and most of their remains consist of stone storage cists and burials in caves, but after that date numerous villages are found, and true pottery began to be made about the same time. This stage, lasting until about A.D. 700, is called the Modified Basketmaker Stage. Subsequent developments are divided for convenience into the following stages:

Developmental Pueblo	A.D. 700 to 1050
Great Pueblo	A.D. 1050 to 1300
Regressive Pueblo	A.D. 1300 to 1700

followed by Historic Pueblo, with which we are not concerned here, lasting until the present day. In this case it is convenient to make an exception to our normal practice and to carry on the story until long after the first contact with the Spaniards, since it did not make a fundamental change in the way of life of the natives as it did in Mexico and Peru. The dates given are approximate, since the stages are not rigidly defined, a particular stage was reached earlier in some areas than in others, and there were many local variations. The stages are marked by developments in house types and pottery decoration, minor changes in such things as utensils, weapons and clothing, and by alterations in the distribution of settlements.

Most of the Modified Basketmaker houses consisted of a wooden framework built over a pit and covered with brush with an outer layer of earth, but surface houses made of vertical poles set close together and plastered with mud began to appear later. The first pottery was plain grey ware, fired in a reducing atmosphere and shaped like gourds or baskets, and some bowls had designs like those on the baskets, painted in black on the inside. The pots were built up at first from rings and then from continuous coils of clay, which were obliterated by scraping while still wet, probably with a piece of gourd, as so often occurs wherever this method of construction is used.

In Developmental Pueblo times, pottery decorated in black over a white slip was introduced. This black-and-white ware is the most characteristic type of Anasazi pottery in Developmental Pueblo times. The use of a slip points to influence from the south, since this trait was common in Mexico, but at this time it was unknown elsewhere in the United States. The use of grey cooking pottery continued, and on the earlier jars and deep bowls the clay rings from which the neck was built were allowed to show, but later examples had an entirely corrugated outside surface consisting of thin constructional coils, which were pinched into a wavy form with striking effect (1). This type continued to the end of Great Pueblo times, after which plain cooking

(1) *Plate* 1.

pots were used. Developmental Pueblo villages consisted of surface houses, first of poles and mud, then of masonry, pit houses being retained for ceremonial purposes. The latter afterwards developed into the circular underground ceremonial chambers known as kivas.

The Great Pueblo Period is marked by the building of great, many-storied houses with hundreds of rooms, sometimes built against overhanging cliffs, sometimes in the open, and by the maximum area of occupation. The Regressive Pueblo Period is so called because the area occupied contracted, and some districts, particularly in the north (S.E. Utah and S.W. Colorado), were abandoned while still apparently in a flourishing condition. The explanation is still uncertain; pestilence, drought, social disturbances, and threats from invading nomads have all been suggested, the latter being perhaps the most probable. At any rate there is nothing decadent about the pottery, in spite of the disturbing influence of the Spaniards after 1540.

Many varieties of black-on-white pottery are found during Developmental and Great Pueblo times. The shapes are comparatively few and simple, consisting of open bowls, bowls with a constricted mouth known as seed jars (1), ladles (2), mugs, and jugs of various forms (called pitchers in America), including an asymmetrical type possibly derived from a bird form (3). The black ornament is executed either with a mineral paint, which is dense and sharp in outline, or with pigment produced by burning vegetable matter, which tends to be rather faint. The designs are essentially geometrical and are either hatched, longitudinally or diagonally, or blacked in (4). There are chequers, rectangles, triangles, stepped triangles, zig-zag bands, bands straight on one side and deeply serrated on the other, frets, spirals, and all sorts of combinations of these and similar motifs. In many cases, black elements are balanced by similar hatched ones, with striking effect (5). In Great Pueblo times, the region has been divided into a number of areas, and the pottery styles of each have distinguishing features. For example, the Chaco area, named after Chaco Canyon in New Mexico, includes a style with elements covered with fine-line diagonal hatching; the Mesa Verde area of south-west Colorado produces vessels with flat, dotted rims and very coarse hatching (5), also flat-bottomed mugs; the Kayenta region of northern Arizona has vessels with elaborate patterns in black, which are so heavy as to make the intermediate white areas appear like negative painting; further south are found the Tularosa wares with their interlocking scroll designs and animal handles (6); and so on.

---

(1) *Plate* 2B; (2) *Plate* 3B; (3) *Plate* 2A; (4) *Plates* 3A, 4A; (5) *Plate* 5B (6) *Plate* 4B.

Alongside the black-on-white wares are found black-on-red ones with similar designs (1), particularly open bowls, and in Great Pueblo times polychrome types are found in some areas. These may be produced by the addition of white to the black-on-red (2), and one type of bowl has black decoration inside and white outside. In the Kayenta area an orange ware with red designs outlined in black is found. A very striking ware was carried into the Gila Basin, part of the Hohokam territory, in the fourteenth century by an Anasazi people whom we call the Salado, having appeared in the Tonto Basin, just to the north, at the end of Great Pueblo times. It consists of large red-slipped jars with bold black and white designs on the outside (3), and simple bowls which generally have a plain red exterior and black designs on a white ground inside.

The Regressive Pueblo Period was one of great changes and remarkable innovations in pottery. There was a great development of polychrome wares and the old black-on-white disappeared. The change from corrugated to plain cooking pots has already been mentioned, but besides the ordinary symmetrical forms they include a peculiar shape, generally called the duck or shoe pot, in which the lower part of the body projects to one side, possibly to facilitate its insertion into the embers of a fire. Plate 7A shows an example which the small protuberances at sides and tail render unusually realistic. Among painted wares, geometrical designs are still found, but stylized life forms, including birds, feathers, insects, animals and masked human figures are much used. Yellow and red backgrounds predominate owing to the use of iron-bearing clays and an oxidizing atmosphere in firing. By far the commonest forms everywhere are bowls and jars.

As in former times there are local styles. An important area is named after the settlement of Hopi in N.E. Arizona, where a black-on-yellow ware, decorated with both geometrical and life forms, developed, by the addition of red, into a most striking ware called Sikyatki Polychrome, with large jars and bowls painted with bold curvilinear designs and stylized birds and feathers. In the Rio Grande area in New Mexico are found numerous varieties of polychrome pottery, most of them of three colours of which one is a brownish-black glaze. The deliberate use of glaze containing lead or copper, for decorative purposes but never for waterproofing, is an innovation characteristic of Regressive Pueblo times, and it continues right through the period in the Rio Grande area. Glaze-painted ware is also found in the Zuñi area in Western New Mexico, from which a number of our illustrations come, but here it was used at the be-

---

(1) *Plate* 5A; (2) *Plate* 6A; (3) *Plate* 6B.

ginning of the period in the fourteenth century and again near the end in the seventeenth century, with a long gap between. In the earlier period, glaze was first used on a red ground, then on a white one together with matt red paint. When it went out of fashion, a succession of matt painted wares took its place. First came a fine yellow ware with red geometrical decoration (1), and at the same time a red ware with rather fugitive white decoration was made. Both were commonly used near Zuñi to contain cremated ashes, when a jar of one ware may have an inverted bowl of the other as a cover. Then comes a well defined polychrome style, which probably developed from the previous red-on-yellow by the addition of black, chiefly used to outline the red (2). At first the ornament was very delicately executed, but it later became coarser and the red areas were sometimes stippled instead of being fully painted. This style lasted until after the second introduction of glaze in the seventeenth century, and some vessel shapes were common to both types of decoration, notably large round-bottomed water jars (3), and bowls of the same profile as the lower part of the jars. The polychrome bowls may be decorated inside with bold designs based on stylized feathers, recalling the Sikyatki ones. The glaze, which is difficult to handle and tends to run, was very crudely applied, much less skilfully than in the earlier period.

With the reconquest of the Pueblo area by the Spaniards in the 1690s, after the great rebellion of 1680, our period comes to an end.

The Hohokam

The Hohokam lived in the Gila and Salt valleys in Arizona from about the beginning of the Christian era until about 1400, after which we have no certain knowledge of them, though they may have been the ancestors of the modern Pima and Papago. Their area is a desert, and it was only by the development of irrigation that they were able to build up a considerable civilization there. This differed in many ways from that of the Anasazi, and had many more features in common with Mexico. Among these were courts for ball games similar to those played by the Maya and other Central American peoples, and the making of large quantities of pottery figurines, generally representing nude women, for religious purposes. For most of their history their houses were single units, slightly sunk in the ground, but they began to build groups of rooms within an enclosing wall late in their history. They cremated their dead, unlike the Anasazi among whom the practice was absent until Regressive Pueblo times. They were skilled

---

(1) *Plate* 7B; (2) *Plate* 8A; (3) *Plate* 8B.

workers in stone, and made stone bowls and palettes with elaborately carved borders, which were frequently buried with the dead. It is believed that they were dependent on flood irrigation until about A.D. 600, after which they constructed an ever-growing canal system, which must have needed an elaborate organization of labour to maintain no less than to build it.

Apart from some early wares with a grey background, the painted pottery of the Hohokam is buff in colour with red decoration, a combination which is as characteristic of them as the black-on-white is of the Anasazi. It was apparently built up of broad bands of clay, but is finished by the paddle and anvil method, in which the walls of the vessel are thinned and shaped by beating them with a wooden paddle against a mushroom-shaped anvil held against the inside, which disguises the original structure. The commonest forms are bowls and jars of various shapes, but in later times, after A.D. 900, tripods, ladles and other forms were added. During what is called the Colonial Period, A.D. 600–900, vessels were frequently painted with small elements, such as birds or animals, repeated over most of the surface but sometimes divided into zones and bordered by bands of diagonal hatching. Spirals are also common. In the subsequent Sedentary Period, A.D. 900–1200, elaborate geometrical designs are also found, giving the effect of plaiting or weaving (1). A very typical form is a large dome-shaped jar with a small mouth and everted lip, with the wall meeting a gently-curved base in a sharp angle called the Gila shoulder (1). After this period the typical arts of the Hohokam declined and red-on-buff pottery became rare. Between 1300 and 1400, the Salado people brought in their black and white on red ware, already mentioned. Their invasion is a very remarkable phenomenon, since they came to the Hohokam villages, where they lived peacefully in their own houses and practised their own crafts, at the same time helping the Hohokam to expand their canal system to the maximum. After about a century, they left as quietly as they had come, and little or nothing more is heard either of them or of the Hohokam.

The Mogollon

The Mogollon area was inhabited by A.D. 300 at the latest, but its pottery was not at first particularly notable and we are not concerned with it until about 1000, when outside influences, mainly Anasazi, combined with the local traditions to produce a very distinctive and beautiful style known as Mimbres black-on-white, though the black

(1) *Plate* 9.

may be replaced by dark brown. The vessels were generally open bowls with the designs painted inside, and most of them come from burials, in which case they were 'killed' by punching a small hole in the middle, which seems to have been done at the graveside since the piece removed is sometimes found in the grave. This custom is particularly common in Mimbres burials, but it is sometimes found elsewhere in the Southwest, including Regressive Pueblo burials in the neighbourhood of Zuñi. The designs fall into two main types, either a broad zone of finely painted geometrical decoration surrounding a blank circle (1), or a few narrow black bands round the top with a lively but conventional representation of an animal or human being at the bottom. These life forms may make up a scene, such as a man fighting a bear, and owing to their position are often marred by the process of 'killing' the bowl. The makers seem to have left the district at about the end of the twelfth century, and it is not certain where they went to, but it is conjectured that some at least may have gone south to the Mexican province of Chihuahua. At any rate a number of Mimbres influences appeared there at that time, followed rather later by features which suggest the arrival of Salado people, including large houses of Salado type. A very distinctive pottery style developed there and flourished until about the middle of the fifteenth century. It is distinguished by crisply painted geometrical designs—triangles, steps, spirals and so on—with occasional life forms, executed in red and black on a buff or white slip. A common form is a deep bowl with rounded base and practically straight sides sloping inwards to the mouth, which has a narrow, slightly everted lip (2). Other shapes include small hemispherical bowls and highly stylized effigy vessels representing human beings or animals. When the Spaniards arrived in the sixteenth century, they found the main Chihuahua sites abandoned. We do not know where the makers of this pottery went or why, but it is not known elsewhere so they must have ceased to make it.

---

(1) *Plate* 10B; (2) *Plate* 10A.

3

THE POTTERY OF CENTRAL AMERICA

To the student accustomed to European forms and decorative techniques, the pottery of Mexico presents a picture at once fascinating in its freshness and originality, and at the same time, daunting in its variety and confusion. Early shapes and decorative techniques recur at intervals in later times and in sites scattered over a wide area. Generalizations are difficult, and in spite of the immense amount of work that has been done, the enormous archaeological heritage of Central America has only been scratched on the surface. It is true that a complete cultural sequence from the earliest times has been established for certain areas—the Valley of Mexico, Monte Alban in Oaxaca, and the Maya regions to the south-east. Several excavations have also been undertaken on the coast of the Gulf of Mexico, and in the west, but the picture is far from complete, even in its outline.

We do know, however, that the various local cultures, with different styles, enjoyed a common historical background, worshipped similar gods, and were linked with their neighbours by trade. New ideas from Teotihuacan, for instance, were soon reflected at Monte Alban, and many traits from the Olmecs became widespread over Mexico. The position was thus very similar to that in Europe today, where we have a common tradition, but where local variations and local emphasis on particular specialities differentiate the products of one country, and even of one manufacturer from those of another.

In the short space available it will be impossible to deal exhaustively with the many and varied developments of central America. We must limit ourselves to the broad outlines and a very inadequate, because over-simplified, picture of the historical developments in America before the Spanish conquest. Archaeologists generally recognize three principal periods. The first, from about 1500 B.C. to about A.D. 300, covering the time when the early Mexicans were emerging from barbarism and developing a simple form of agriculture, is known as the Formative Period. The next, the period of independent cities living under priestly rule, and enjoying, for the most part, the advantages of

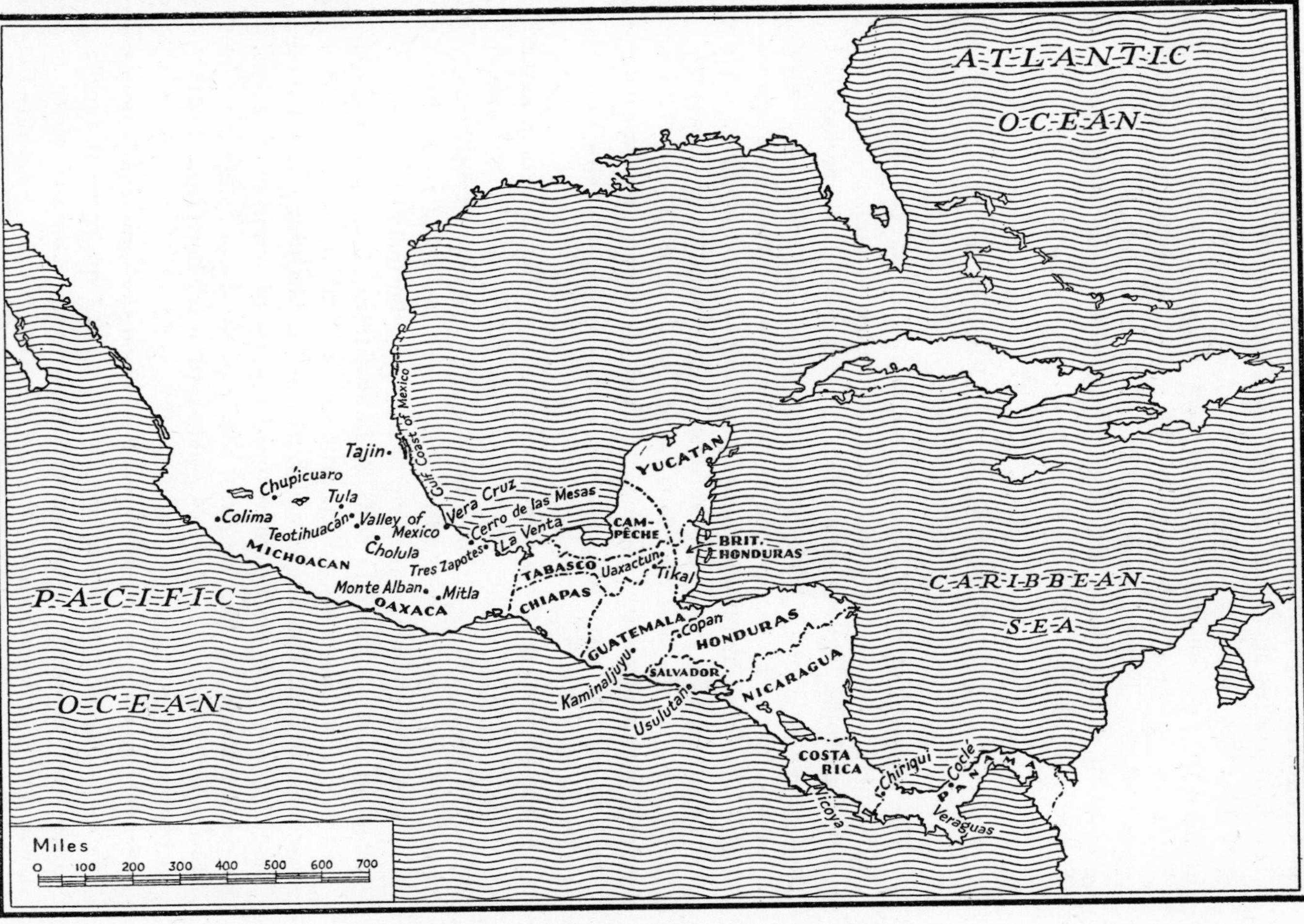

MEXICO AND CENTRAL AMERICA

peace and trade with their neighbours, is known as the Classic Period. This lasted from about A.D. 200 till some time in the tenth century A.D. The final, or Post Classic, period was a very complicated one of tribal wars, and the incursion of barbaric invaders. It saw the fall of Teotihuacan, the abandonment of the old Maya cities, the rise and spread of the Toltecs, their overthrow by new invaders, and the growth of the power of the Aztecs, and their final overthrow by Cortez in 1519–21.

THE FORMATIVE PERIOD
(Approximately 1500 B.C. to A.D. 300)

The earliest pottery of central America was made by people who had emerged from the purely hunting stage of culture, and had started a simple form of agriculture. At the end of the period they had developed many traits which continued into the succeeding 'Classic' Period. Even mounds to support the temples, indicating a highly developed hierarchic civilization, have been found at Formative Period sites such as Cuicuilco in Mexico, Kaminaljuyu in Guatemala and in the Olmec sites on the coast of the Gulf of Mexico. This is especially true of pottery making, for there are hardly any features of the immediately succeeding periods which do not already occur in a crude form at this stage.

At the beginning, as we might expect, simple forms predominated such as plates, hemispherical bowls, wide lipped bowls, and almost spherical storage jars with short necks and everted lips. A rather more ambitious form was a vase with a short upturned spout rather like a teapot. A very characteristic form of the early 'Formative' was the so-called composite silhouette bowl, so-named from an angle low down on the side of the vessel which produced a break in the even curve from base to rim. This angle, which marked the dividing line between base and sides, took on the character of a flange or rim in later vessels, and is obviously the forerunner of the beautiful basal flange bowls of the Classic Period of the Maya. A good example is a bowl from Tlatilco, near Mexico City, illustrated in Plate 11B.

In the later stages of the Formative Period the same fundamental shapes continued with various embellishments. Supports of various kinds were adopted, in particular simple ring bases like those of modern cups or some form of tripod. The tripod support is perhaps the most typical feature of central American pottery, but it lends itself to an almost infinite range of variation. The earliest form in the valley of Mexico was a simple solid cone, which was later improved by being made hollow. In other places, notably on the Gulf coast, they evolved into a swollen mammiform shape. Small nubbins (solid studlike projections), on a flat base seem to have originated somewhere in the southern part of Guatemala. Plain slab supports on cylindrical tripod vases were found at the end of the period in the earliest pottery from the Maya city of Copan.

Clay was used not only for the manufacture of utilitarian vessels. From the earliest times little effigy figurines (1) were modelled by hand with features delicately punched or incised, possibly for use as votive offerings. Later magnificent representations were made in which acute observation was combined with skilful adaptation to the necessities of vessel shape to produce vases of great charm like the fish vase from Tlatilco (2) which is now in the Museo Nacional de Antropologia in Mexico City. Like the vessel forms, surface finish and decorative techniques varied greatly. Plain storage vases were undecorated, but the majority were painted with a slip in one colour (black, brown, red, or white) and burnished. Geometrical patterns in red on a white ground have been found at a number of sites, and black on white from some others. Incising either before or after firing was well known. The earliest patterns were curvilinear but later vessels showed geometrical designs and the use of cross-hatching (3) to fill spaces. The latter is the forerunner of the practice of scraping away the slip to produce a pattern emphasized by the differing colours of the slip and paste of the vessel, which became typical of many of the Teotihuacan vases of the 'Classic' Period. Another unusual decorative technique, shared with South America, is 'negative painting', in which the design is painted in hot wax or some similar substance and then given an all-over coat of paint, after which the wax is removed, leaving the design in the original colour of the vessel. A variant of this, known as the Usulutan technique from a site in Salvador, is widespread in the last phases of the 'Formative' Period. Polychrome pottery came in at about the same time. The earliest form, from Cerro de las Mesas in the State of Vera Cruz, was not a true polychrome in so far as only two paints were used; the bare clay of the vessel provided the third colour.

The Maya

The Maya, whose earliest cities were at Tikal and Uaxactun in the lowland area of the Peten, developed, like the peoples of central Mexico, out of the Formative culture phase, but were subject to influences from an unknown source probably to the south of them. Their 'Formative' Period (known as 'Mamom' and 'Chicanel', earlier and

(1) *Plate* 11A and B; (2) *Plate* 12; (3) *Plate* 13.

later respectively) carried most of the traits found elsewhere but lacked punctate ornament and the use of incising to outline zones of colour. The commonest domestic vessel was a large almost spherical storage jar with short neck and everted lip. This was to persist right through the whole of the Classic Period of the Maya with only slight modifications. A coat of coloured clay slip was applied to the better wares—black, red, or orange. Black-ware shapes were, in the earlier Mamom phase, a jar with incised ornament, and in the later Chicanel phase, basal flange bowls, either with ring bases or *cascabel* feet (that is to say, hollow feet with small clay pellets inside, which rattled when moved). Red-slipped plates with flaring sides and bowls, both with horizontal grooving, occurred in the Mamom; in the Chicanel phase, the plates had a wide everted lip and the bowls had a thickened lip curving outwards. The only orange-ware shape was a bowl which occurred in the Mamom phase.

THE CLASSIC PERIOD

(Approximately A.D. 300–A.D. 980)

This term is used to cover the long period which saw the growth and full florescence of the big independent ceremonial cities. It was a period devoted to the service of the gods and to the study of astronomy, marked by priestly domination of the peasant population; the building of great temples and pyramids; and the development of the arts of sculpture, pottery and painting for ritual purposes. It was a period of peace and established order on the whole, in which trade flourished exceedingly. There was a common basic culture, but each of the large centres or regions retained its individuality and specialized not only in artistic style but also in differing aspects of technical and social emphasis. In central Mexico the most important were Teotihuacan, Monte Alban, the home of the Zapotecs in Oaxaca, and Cholula. To the south-east in Chiapas, Yucatan, Guatemala and Honduras was the Maya culture, with its special concentration on astronomical problems. On the Gulf coast the Olmecs continued, and other peoples such as the Huaxtec and Totonac were developing. In western Mexico, despite several important excavations in recent years, it is still very difficult to form a clear picture; but the general impression we get is one of a continuation of the traditions of the Formative culture with certain rather specialized wares, to which we are unable at the moment to assign any definite position. These will be discussed later (pp. 19 and 20).

MEXICAN HIGHLANDS

The period is best exemplified in central Mexico by the site of Teotihuacan. Here the earliest vessels were similar to those of the

Formative Period. In the early phases of the second, or 'Classic' Period, which was one of development and experiment, pottery was universally monochrome. The most typical form was a flat-based globular vase, with, to European eyes, a disproportionately large flaring neck (1). The colour varied from black to grey or chocolate. Decoration consisted of a number of parallel or intersecting lines produced by smoothing or lightly scraping the surface. More elaborate vases of this type frequently bore a face modelled in relief, probably representing a god. The more elaborate clearly depicted Tlaloc, the rain-god (2). Other forms were an ewer with a conical neck, vases with one or two vertical spouts supported by struts to the neck, and a pleasing little vase known locally as a *florero*, or flower vase. This has a very small bulbous body and a tall trumpetlike neck (3). There were also plates very similar to a modern soup-plate and flat-based flaring bowls with three very small nubbin feet. The whole of this phase which must have lasted about three hundred years is essentially uninspiring so far as the pottery is concerned. This is, no doubt, the result of emphasis on building, and also reflects the struggles of a developing civilization against both man and nature.

The succeeding phase is, by contrast, rich and colourful, many new shapes and techniques being employed. It is as if the Teotihuacanos had at last attained a golden age of peace and prosperity in which their energies were diverted to the arts and craftsmen had time to learn from their neighbours and to experiment with new techniques. Perhaps the most remarkable is that known as *fresco* or *cloisonné poterie* (4). In this the whole surface of a vessel was covered with a thin film of coloured plaster. The greater part of this was cut away, leaving thin walls to form partitions between the plaster of other colours which was then applied to the intervening spaces. After smoothing the surface presented a clean design with no smeared edges or running colours. Pastel shades were used, generally blue, green, pink and white. Of course this remarkable technique suffered from the disadvantage of being very fragile, and it was technically unsound. Examples have been found at many sites, but they are very rare, and undamaged specimens are almost if not quite unknown. Allied to this technique, but probably rather more recent, is that known as champlevé. In this the black or dark brown slip is scraped or cut away, leaving the design in low relief; and the scraped background is then filled in or painted with cinnabar (5).

The moulded figurines are very well made and some of great beauty, but all are characterized by over elaboration and great atten-

(1) *Plate* 14; (2) *Plate* 15; (3) *Plate* 17B; (4) *Plate* 16; (5) *Plate* 17D.

tion to iconographic detail. They are an indication of the number of the gods they worshipped even more perhaps than the richness of their apparel. But some time after A.D. 700 the last phase of Teotihuacan began, and a decline set in. The figurines, which are our best guide, show a coarsening of workmanship. Detail is still provided by moulded elements, but this is combined with modelling similar to that of the Formative Period, without its artistic merit. Very little is known of the ordinary pottery of the phase. Obviously a long lived and exhausted civilization was tottering to its fall. New peoples appeared, the vigorous Nahua speakers, whose forerunners were the Toltecs of Tula, a city some few miles northwards. They seem to have caused the downfall of Teotihuacan and to have set in motion a chain reaction which spread through the whole of central America. This was the end of the classic age of central America. But before we go on to consider the Post-Classic Period, we must retrace our steps to look at the pottery of the people who were contemporaries of the Teotihuacanos. Outside the valley of Mexico, but still sufficiently near to be influenced from it, was the city of Cholula, whose history ran from the Formative Period right down to the Spanish conquest. But for the most part, pottery made here seemed to follow the styles of the valley. At first it resembled the Formative and Teotihuacan and later, the polychrome trade wares of Sacrificios and Tlascala. But towards the end of the Teotihuacan phase a definite local style developed. Typical of it were little narrow-necked vases of red or coffee-coloured clay, flat plates with wavy line ornament, and hemispherical bowls with an ornamental border of red or black fringelike painting on a yellow ground.

But the real area of development independent of the Mexican Highlands was in the territory of the Maya, who occupied the south-eastern provinces of Mexico, Guatemala, Honduras, and British Honduras.

The Maya

The Classic Period among the Maya was roughly contemporaneous with Teotihuacan. During this period the Maya reached greater intellectual heights than any other people in central America. Their most outstanding achievements were in the realms of astronomy and mathematics. Not unnaturally the elaborate hieroglyphic script and the beautiful carving of the stelae they erected to record the passage of time were reflected in the painting of the pottery, though there was much borrowing from other sources.

For ritual purposes the simpler wares of the Formative Period were replaced by a fully fledged polychrome ware known as Tzakol, generally with a cream or orange coloured base on which are painted designs in red and black. There are also negative designs painted in the Usulutan technique, by a wax resist, which was allowed to run, and occasional examples of stucco or 'fresco' vessels rather like those from the valley of Mexico. Shapes may be summarized as plates and basal-flanged and other types of bowls. Perhaps the most characteristic forms were a subspherical bowl with a flattened base, and bowls with straight or slightly curved flaring sides. The basal-flanged bowls fall into two groups, those with a ring base (1), and those with a number of mammiform feet. In America vases usually have three feet, but in the early classic phase, four footed vases were not uncommon. It is generally believed that they were introduced from somewhere in the south. Tetrapod feet, especially bulbous, were found not only in the Tepeu phase of the Maya Classic Period but also at La Venta, in the Olmec territory on the Gulf coast, and at Monte Alban in the state of Oaxaca. As we shall see later Monte Alban was much influenced by the Maya as well as from Teotihuacan.

Decoration on the plain unslipped vases and dishes took the form of incising and the application of pellets, some of them conical in shape, giving almost a spiny appearance to some of the vessels. Incising of black ware and scraping away areas of the surface to reveal the orange coloured paste is so reminiscent of the third phase of Teotihuacan that it is hard to believe that the idea did not come from a common source. The polychrome decoration of this early Classic phase was geometrical or at least highly conventionalized. It varied from bands of black and red often divided by a wavy line, through a rich variety of rectangles, steps and frets (2) to conventionalized serpents set in panels. The insides of plates and dishes were painted as well as the outsides, decoration generally taking the form of animals such as the jaguar, or sometimes fish (3).

The second part of the Classic Period of the Maya, known as the Tepeu phase, which corresponded to the greatest period of their architecture and astronomy, was one of great variety. The most characteristic shape was a tall cylindrical vase, slightly bulbous, or convex, or with straight sides. Most have tripod feet, either hollow cones or slabs. Other shapes were flaring-sided dishes and bowls with or without basal flanges. Tripod feet, when found, are often cylindrical. Tetrapod bowls were no longer made. There were of course marginal variants. Pusilha in British Honduras, produced a polychrome bowl

(1) *Plate* 19A; (2) *Plate* 18A; (3) *Plate* 19B.

with an intertwined bud pattern; and at the very end of the period, San José in the same colony produced a trumpet-shaped pedestal base. Plain grey- or red-slipped vessels were found, but the most spectacular were the polychrome vessels and a monochrome ware in which the ornament was carved in low relief (1). The designs on the carved vessels was usually limited to a narrow band of hieroglyphs, sometimes so conventionalized so far as to be unrecognizable and almost always meaningless (2). They were used purely for ornament, and not as inscriptions. Indeed it seems that they were carved or painted by people entirely ignorant of their meaning, which was only known to a learned few. Other decoration consisted of bands or panels showing scenes from Maya ceremonial life. Polychrome painted ornament had the same arrangement of meaningless glyphs, sometimes in conjunction with panels and conventionalized animals. Geometrical and cursive patterns were also common. But the most beautiful of all were painted scenes depicting Maya ceremonial life (3).

The Zapotecs

Monte Alban in the province of Oaxaca lies south from the valley of Mexico, and westwards from the Maya area. It was the home of the Zapotecs, and like the other cultures we have discussed, had its roots in the Formative Period. A flourishing city had grown up with features derived both from the Maya and the Teotihuacanos, as well as from the Olmec region on the Gulf coast. Pottery was no exception and we can detect both influences in the second phase of Monte Alban which was the first phase of the Classic Period (4). Here as elsewhere, many of the Formative shapes survived. The new features of the period were the use of dull greyish slips like those of Teotihuacan; 'fresco' and painting, and scraped decoration, suggesting the same source; globular and mammiform supports (5), generally tetrapod; and waisted potstands probably derived from the Maya. Also within the scope of their potters were large effigy urns, which were placed in their tombs. Sometimes these took the form of a bat god (6), sometimes of the rain god (7), or of almost any other god in the Zapotec pantheon. The third phase of Monte Alban corresponds to the late Classic phases elsewhere and there was a similar richness of the arts. The funerary urns, like the figurines of Teotihuacan, became more elaborate to satisfy the requirements of iconographic detail and to reflect the growing elaboration of their ceremonial clothing. At the beginning of the third phase the pottery seemed to show more contact

(1) *Plate* 20; (2) *Plate* 18B; (3) *Plate* 21 *and Colour Plate* B; (4) *Plate* 22; (5) *Plate* 23; (6) *Plate* 24; (7) *Plate* 25.

B. *Polychrome bowl, Maya, late classic 9th or 10th century* A.D., *from Guatemala. Height* 5¾ *in. British Museum*
(*See p.* 16)

with Teotihuacan in that *floreros*, vases with two vertical spouts, and cups with a suggestion of the style of the Teotihuacan predominated. A dull grey slip still continued with frequent use of scraped ornament. In the later part of this phase the use of engraved or scraped ornament declined. Some of the Teotihuacan forms went out of use and the urns became even more elaborate. This was the high watermark of the Zapotec culture at Monte Alban. A confused and rather degenerate phase followed, no doubt because the Zapotecs were feeling the pressure of their Mixtec neighbours to whom they were soon to abandon their city.

The Coast of the Gulf of Mexico

The inhabitants of the low-lying country on the Gulf of Mexico were of a physical type more closely linked to the Maya than to the dwellers in the Highlands of central Mexico, but their early pottery of the Formative Period conforms generally to that in other places, and there was undoubtedly a great deal of cultural give and take between the two areas. This can be recognized in the very beautiful *florero* from Cerro de las Mesas (1). Research in this region is comparatively recent, and we have not had sufficient time to evaluate all the archaeological evidence, and form a completely satisfying interpretation of it. In the earlier upper layers at Cerro de las Mesas polychrome vessels are very frequent, often resembling the polychrome of Cholula. Other forms include little vases with moulded ornament applied to the bottoms and sides.

Western Mexico
(Dating uncertain)

To the west of Mexico, in the state of Michoacan and further west on the Pacific coast, are a number of isolated cultures which it is hard to equate with the main stream of development. In the extreme west there is the well known culture of Colima where the artistic traditions of the Formative Period seem to have established themselves firmly and developed to some extent on their own lines. Small figurines (2), typically Formative in feeling and technique, though painted red or red on white, are the most characteristic products; but larger and probably later examples, in human or animal form were made in quantities. The whole art of Colima differs from that of the valley of Mexico and from the Maya in the lighthearted way the potters of the areas portrayed—one might almost say caricatured—warriors or religious dignitaries, and almost in the same breath modelled the most

(1) *Plate* 26; (2) *Plate* 27.

charming effigies of the little fat dogs of the region (1). The only other example of an outlook on life which escaped from a general atmosphere of earnestness is found in the so-called laughing heads of the Totonacs on the other side of Mexico. Pottery seems to have followed the general lines of the Classic Period but with greater freedom and more variety. Much of it is beautifully made, owing its inspiration to natural forms. A striking innovation for the area was the use, not only of spouts like teapots, but of stirrup spouts comparable with those of Peru but much more slender.

In the state of Guanajuato, a somewhat similar picture is portrayed by the finds from Chupícuaro. Here were produced pleasing figurines, rather flatter than most but with features indicated by fillets of clay neatly applied to form slanting eyes. These are often rather loosely termed the 'pretty lady' type (2), and are neither slipped nor painted. But a later type, which is probably contemporary with the early polychrome wares of the Classic Period, is painted with rather tightly drawn geometrical patterns in red, white and black. The same style of decoration is found on the vessels, where the black either forms a boundary between the red and white areas (3), or appears as cross-hatching in the white. There is a great variety of vessel forms; plates, triangular bowls, cups, and dishes, often on large tripod supports (4) or trumpet-shaped pedestal bases. The walls of these vessels are always thick and with rounded edges giving an impression of massiveness and solidity rather than delicacy of workmanship.

THE POST CLASSIC PERIOD
(*Including the Final Period*)
(A.D. 980–A.D. 1521)

It is convenient to date the end of the Classic, and the beginning of the Post Classic Period with the destruction of Teotihuacan and the founding in 980 of Tula, the principal city of the Toltecs. The arrival of the Toltecs ushered in a period of savage warfare and ended the long period of relatively peaceful hierarchic rule under which individual communities had evolved their own local styles and affected their neighbours by trade. The Toltecs' influence spread far and wide, but even beyond it a great upheaval was in progress. Strongly individualistic local styles seem to have suffered an eclipse, if only temporary in some cases, and three broad types of pottery seem to have held the chief place in the better known sites for a while.

The earliest ware found at Tula was a polished brown or buff ware with red painted ornament. The most typical form was a heavily

(1) *Plate* 28; (2) *Plate* 29A; (3) *Plate* 29B; (4) *Plate* 30.

built tripod with legs of an almost conical shape. These do not have the appearance of being made separately and attached to the vessel as is the case with most American tripod supports; but rather of being made integrally with it, for the curving outline of the legs seems to blend without any break of line into the general form of the bowl. This type has been found as far west as Chupícuaro; intermittently through western Mexican sites; then again at Isla de Sacrificio and neighbouring sites on the Gulf of Mexico. It seems to have been a kind of forerunner to the Mazápan style of pottery. Mazápan pottery is also a ware with red decoration on buff (1). The absolutely unmistakable characteristic of it is the use of parallel wavy lines as the only motive of decoration used. Shapes include plates with tripod supports, jars, cylindrical vases, bowls and biconical cups. The third main type at the beginning of the Toltec period is the pottery known as Coyotlatelco ware. This is very similar to the pottery found at Matlatzinca in the state of Michoacan (2). The principal forms are a hemispherical bowl, and a flaring-sided bowl with a flat base. Both of these have tripod supports. There is also a flattened bowl very much resembling a rather flattened pudding basin. Decoration on these vessels consists of red bands, frets, and scrolls in a pleasing mixture of thick and narrow lines painted in red on a cream background. When the main decoration is on the inside, either the rim is painted or there is a broad band of red on the outside near the base. Allied to this ware, in shape at any rate, are a number of flaring-sided tripod bowls of a polished coffee colour in which the decoration consists of a wide red band further embellished by incised geometrical or scroll patterns. There are examples of negative painting and many other styles of decoration.

We must now turn our attention to two very important types of pottery, made in large quantities and traded wherever Toltec influence was felt. They are 'Fine Orange' ware, so-called because it is made from a singularly fine-grained paste of an orange colour, and 'Plumbate'.

FINE ORANGE WARE

The distinguishing feature of 'Fine Orange' is that, while almost every other ware in Central America has some form of tempering medium such as sand, calcite, tuff, or ground-down potsherds, there is none in 'Fine Orange'. There are two varieties, which have been labelled X and Z for convenience. In both, the paste is of an even colour throughout, of fine texture, with a china-like fracture; but where the surface of X is rather hard and lustrous and rather harsh to the touch, Z is smooth, chalky and matt, and frequently has a red or white slip.

---

(1) *Plate* 31A; (2) *Plate* 31B.

The commoner forms of Z seem to be limited to open spheroid or paraboloid bowls; while X-type forms include cylindrical, pear-shaped, and globular jars with either tripod or trumpet-shaped pedestal bases, and most forms of bowl known to central America. There are examples of incised ornament in the Z style, usually in the form of a scroll band round the outside of bowls from Yucatan. There are so many variants of the decoration of fine orange pottery, and so many shapes which seem to belong to the different localities in which they were found, that we are tempted to put forward, with all possible reserve, the tentative suggestion that the trade was not in finished pottery but in the raw material—the clay—which seems to be the only unifying factor, common to all examples of this ware. Generally speaking it seems to be commonest in the south and east of Mexico and the probable centre of origin was somewhere in the Totonac country.

Plumbate Ware

Apparently contemporary with Fine Orange ware was the so-called plumbate pottery, which is probably the most remarkable ware in central America. It is hard and well fired in an area where all other wares are relatively soft, and differs from nearly all other wares of its time by relying on a lustrous appearance and on incised ornament for its attractive qualities when other wares tended to depend on a fine finish and the skilled use of polychrome painting. It was essentially a monochrome ware, with a colour variation from greyish black to dark olive. Ornament was incised before the application of the slip, and took the flamboyant form so familiar in the art of the Toltec period. Vessel shapes were numerous. The simpler and earlier forms resembled an *olla*. Bulbous jars with wide, deep and flaring necks (1) were common; and towards the end of the period cylindrical vases with flat or rounded bases were made. Variations of these were waisted, barrel-shaped or piriform. Gadrooning occurred on a number of vessels. Often the figures of gods or animals were luted onto the sides of the vases; or whole vessels might be made in the effigy of an animal or bird. Many of the shapes described above were modified to stand on pedestal bases or on mammiform cascabel tripod supports. An effigy vase is shown in (2). Finish and workmanship are extremely poor and careless. Vases are seldom symmetrical. Small fragments of clay distributed by the incising tool are left standing, and accidental roughness in the paste is not smoothed out, but simply covered with a thick slip. The name Plumbate suggests an admixture of lead to the

---

(1) *Plate* 39; (2) *Plate* 33.

clay to produce the semblance of a glaze, but the term is a misnomer. Several factors, many of them fortuitous, contributed to the lustrous finish. By far the most important were the high temperature of firing, in the neighbourhood of 950° Centigrade, in a reducing furnace; and the use of a very specialized form of clay. The variation of colour is due to the difficulty of controlling the amount of oxygen in the fire under primitive conditions. The lustre, it is suggested, is due to the two coats of slip, which may have fired differently.

It is fairly clear from the archaeological associations that Plumbate ware dates from about A.D. 1000, but we cannot say with any certainty where it originated. Examples have been found as far afield as Tola in Nicaragua and the Chiriquí province of Panama in the south; Tula and Teotihuacan in central Mexico; and various sites in Yucatan. But the greatest density of sites occurs on the Pacific slopes of Guatemala, and in Salvador. The place of its origin must have been somewhere on the west coast. From its distribution we can say that Plumbate was a trade ware.

The manufacture is plausibly assigned to some wandering band of Nahua-speaking immigrants, who stumbled upon a deposit of clay having peculiar qualities which they exploited to the full. But in comparison with pottery previously made by Nahua speakers, the ware shows a decline in artistic quality. The potters seem to have lost their artistic sensibility; and to have replaced the careful workmanship and skilful use of colour which characterized the early wares by an orgy of over-elaborate decoration and bad workmanship, redeemed to some extent by the hardness and durability of the paste and by better firing methods. The flamboyance and over-elaboration of the incised ornament of many specimens of this ware can only be rivalled by some of our own products of the Victorian era. But like the Victorian manufactures, also products of high technical quality, they secured a very wide market, and are found in archaeological sites throughout central America.

THE FINAL PERIOD (1325–1521)

The Final Period of pre-Columbian history in central America is that in which the Aztecs after 1325[1] emerged from the welter of warring tribes and gradually became the dominant power. Pottery in this period is extremely varied in both shape and style of decoration, as all the local styles were brought to Tenochtitlan by processes of war and trade.

[1] The date of the founding of Tenochtitlan (Mexico City) has been taken arbitrarily as the beginning of the final period of Pre-Columbian archaeology in Central America.

Black on Orange Pottery

This ware is generally known as Aztec, though its early forms were found long before the rise of the Aztecs, at sites such as Tula or Coyotlatelco. But later examples are very common in Tenochtitlan. It is yellowish or orange in colour, unpolished, well fired and rather thin with ornament painted in the form of very thin lined geometrical, or concentric patterns (1). The concentric ornament became finer in execution and finally gave place in Late Aztec times to naturalistic bird, animal and floral patterns in very thin black lines embellished with thicker areas of red. Forms embraced the usual range of plates and bowls with or without tripod supports which themselves fell into two types, narrow, conical and almost hornlike, or flat and slablike, sometimes with stepped sides. One special form was an elongated dish with a depression at one end, possibly intended for the collection of gravy or blood (2). Many of the bowls had the floors roughened by sharp criss-cross incising to form a grater for some form of soft grain (3). Miniature tripod bowls, about two inches in diameter were used to rest the points of spindles in when spinning cotton (4).

Late Aztec

(A.D. 1400–A.D. 1521)

Cups of two shapes, either biconical (5) or with incurving sides on a tall pedestal base (6) were made for the use of the old men drinking pulque, the fermented juice of the maguey, which was forbidden to the young. They were made thicker than the orange ware, painted red, polished and ornamented with black conventional designs sometimes picked out with incising. The ornament of the biconical form is in parallel lines, usually in black but sometimes in black and white.

In the last Aztec phase were made bichrome bowls, either red on white or black on red (7), and ewers with the same colour.

Mixteca Puebla Pottery and Other Imported Wares

From the Mixtec country in Oaxaca there came in late Aztec times a beautiful highly polished polychrome pottery ornamented with a variety of motives, human figures similar to those in the codices, religious and secular symbols, feathers, scrolls, and so on. A very rare form of this ware is the incense burner (8) but the characteristic shapes were a globular vase with a wide mouth and low neck set on tripod supports (9) and small ewers (10) in which the handle was

(1) *Plate* 35B; (2) *Plate* 34A; (3) *Plate* 34B; (4) *Plate* 35A; (5) *Plate* 36B; (6) *Plate* 37B; (7) *Plates* 36A, 37A; (8) *Plate* 40; (9) *Plate* 38; (10) *Plate* 39.

sometimes hollow and served as a spout. There is one example of a cylindrical tripod vase in the British Museum, but the type is very rare. Very similar is the pottery from Tlascala and Cholula, where the common shape is an incurving bowl usually mounted on a pedestal (1). This ware had the same highly polished surface and brilliantly coloured ornament, but the designs were usually of a geometrical character, and often concentrated in a wide band near the rim.

From further afield in the State of Vera Cruz comes a globular bowl with a yellow slip on which two enormous centipedes have been incised and painted in red (2).

Other Late Pottery from Eastern Mexico

The State of Vera Cruz always seems to have had a rather independent approach to the manufacture of pottery and in the Post-Classic period this is true of the pottery of the Huaxtecs and of the Totonacs. Pottery made by the former bears a white slip with conventional designs heavily painted in black. Forms include small effigy vases with the human form represented partly in relief and partly in black paint; plates; and a curious vessel rather like a teapot which was probably used for the serving of hot chocolate (3). The general impression left by this ware is one of coarseness, irregularity and unbalanced proportions. In striking contrast to this is the Totonac pottery, quantities of which have been found on the Island of Sacrificios in the Gulf of Mexico. This is well made and well fired ware with a sandy buff coloured paste, decorated with geometrical forms in white and brown or black with the white predominating. Frets and step patterns occur, as do naturalistic forms; for example, shells or skulls, in the centre of plates. The most general impression, however, is of broad horizontal bands of white interrupted at short intervals, and picked out with very thin bands of black or brown and varied by pleasing curls and scrolls. Shapes include plates, sometimes supported on tripods, bowls, globular, narrow-necked vases, and tall cylindrical vases on conical pedestal bases (4). The last are decorated with vertical stripes of white and black in equal width. Their paste is reminiscent of Fine Orange ware, and may indeed in some cases be the same.

Pottery of Nicaragua, Costa Rica, and Panama
(Dating uncertain)

The southern part of central America, embracing the states of Nicaragua, Costa Rica, and Panama, is not so well known archaeo-

(1) *Plate* 41; (2) *Plate* 42; (3) *Plate* 43B; (4) *Plates* 44A and B, 45.

logically as Mexico and the Maya area. Dating of the various finds is not properly understood and it is an area of great confusion, being influenced by both Nahua and Maya speaking cultures from the north and by various cultures from South America. In this section therefore the material will be treated on a typological basis and only incidental reference will be made to the chronological aspect.

The first group we shall consider, and possibly the first in point of time, is that found at Chiriqui and as a trade ware in Veraguas in Panama. It is named Biscuit ware by Holmes, and Armadillo ware by McCurdy, after the predominant animal prototype for the relief decoration which adorns it. But since human, monkey, fish and bird forms also occur in quantity, the term seems unduly restricted. Biscuit is the more convenient term and has the advantage of being accurately descriptive (1). In appearance this pottery bears a very close resemblance to modern European pottery after its first firing and before glazing, when it is technically known as biscuit. The commonest shapes are fairly wide high-shouldered vases with a comparatively short neck. Other forms include bowls and dishes of various shapes. Any of them may be modified by the presence of pedestal bases or wide hollow tripod supports containing pellets to serve as rattles. Handles springing from the neck are also common. Ornament is either modelled in full relief or in appliqué in the form of conventionalized parts of an armadillo, or less often of some other animal or fish. Very rarely vessels are modelled completely in the form of an armadillo. The great attraction of the ware lies in the beautiful proportions and excellent workmanship. These are shown to great advantage by the light even sandy colour, which is hardly ever marred by the 'firing clouds' which spoil so much of the monochrome pottery of America. Closely allied to the Biscuit ware of Chiriqui, so far as texture is concerned, are the vessels from the Highlands of Costa Rica and Nicaragua, ornamented with incising and appliqué figures, and frequently on tall hollow tripod supports. Vessels of similar shapes, ornamented by negative painting (2), or by conventionalized alligator designs (3), often reduced to mere bands of triangles were also made.

There are many other monochrome wares in the area, chiefly of red, brown, or black colour, often ornamented with simple incised designs or with simple painting in one colour on the natural surface of the paste. The only major wares which remain to be considered are the polychrome pottery of Coclé in Panama and the so-called Nicoya polychrome pottery of Nicaragua. Both these wares had many variations in shape and style of decoration. The commonest shapes from

(1) *Plate* 46B; (2) *Plate* 47A; (3) *Pltae* 47B.

C. *Polychrome pedestal dish from Coclé, Panama, 14th century* A.D.
Diam. 11 *in.*
Cambridge University Museum of Archaeology and Ethnology
(*See p.* 26)

Coclé were plates, circular or rectangular, on ring bases. Other forms were open bowls, and carafes with either rounded or angular shoulders and inverted subconical necks. Spouted vases, similar to those in Mexico, and effigy vessels were also made in great variety. The decorations were generally in the form of heavy scrolls, outlined in bold black lines with a red filling on a cream base, and various zoomorphic designs arranged symmetrically (1). It has been dated by Dr. Lothrop as being about 200 years earlier than the Spanish conquest.

Nicoya polychrome ware is also characterized by many variations both in shape and style of decoration. This might well be expected, since it is a blend of widely spread influences—Nahua, Maya and South America. Dating of this ware is uncertain, but it probably belongs to the Post Classic period. The commonest basic forms are egg-shaped vessels, and large pear-shaped vases (2). They may be supported on a heavily made ring base, or on tripod supports, which are often elaborately modelled in the form of animal heads, and are generally much bigger than similar supports in Mexico. Other forms include bowls, cups and dishes which may be modified by similar supports. A large number may have attached to them heads, limbs and tails of animals, generally modelled in relief (3), though often the limbs are indicated only by painting. The overall slip of these pots varies in colour from a very deep cream (almost an orange colour), to a very pale almost off-white. Painted designs are generally in red or orange with black outlines, sometimes in black alone. The fauna which form the elements of these designs include turkeys and other birds, frogs, and many creatures which are too conventionalized to identify. Some designs are purely conventional and geometric. Monkeys, jaguars, plumed serpents and figures of Gods bear witness to the influence from the Maya Territory and from the Mexican Highlands. But though the decorative motives show different origins, and a variety of detail which almost defies classification, there is a fundamental unity about Nicoya Polychrome pottery. The heaviness and size of the base and the elaboration of the tripod supports, combined with an intangible quality in the contours of the vessels, are no doubt the features which most surely mark this pottery as being apart from all other central American wares.

---

(1) *Colour Plate* C; (2) *Plate* 48; (3) *Plate* 49B.

THE CENTRAL ANDES

Simplified table indicating approximate dates and area of occurrence of cultures named in the text.

	NORTH		CENTRE		SOUTH	
	Highlands	*Coast*	*Highlands*	*Coast*	*Highlands*	*Coast*
A.D. 1532						
	Inca	Inca	Inca	Inca	Inca	Inca
1450						
		Chimu		Chancay		Ica
1200						
		Huari	Huari	Huari	Tiahuanaco	Huari
1000						
	Recuay	Mochica	Huari		Tiahuanaco Pucára	Nazca
A.D. / B.C. 1						
						Paracas } Cavernas }
400						
	Chavin	Cupisnique		Chavin		
B.C. 800						

THE CENTRAL ANDES
and adjacent region
Chimborazo
Guayaquil
Puná
ECUADOR
BRAZIL
HIGHLANDS
R. Chicama
Chanchan
Trujillo
Chavin
PERU
R. Chancay
Lima
Huari
Cuzco
Paracas
Ica
Nazca
Lake Titicaca
Tiahuanaco
BOLIVIA
PACIFIC
OCEAN
CHILE
ARGENT-INA
Miles
0 50 100 200 300 400 500 600

4

SOUTH AMERICA

The chief archaeological remains in South America are found in the mountainous areas in the west and on the west coast, and within this part of the continent the central Andean region, comprising highland Peru and Bolivia and the coast of Peru, was the home of the highest ancient civilizations. More is known of them than of the less important ones of Colombia, Ecuador, north Chile or north-west Argentina. In each of these countries, a highly diversified topography, with consequent differences in climate, resulted in the growth of many tribes or small nations, and many varieties of material products, of which pottery was not the least. Not until the fifteenth century did the rise of the Inca Empire weld the peoples of Peru and the neighbouring countries into a coherent whole, and even then Colombia and much of the coast of Ecuador remained as before.

A feature of the archaeology of this region, which distinguishes it from Mexico, is that there are few signs of the trade in finished objects between different areas though there is plenty of evidence for exchanges of raw materials. For example, wool from the Peruvian highlands was abundantly used in coastal textiles, and metals from the highlands were made into vessels, tools and ornaments on the coast. Even where certain decorative methods and motifs in pottery, textiles and carvings were sufficiently widespread to be called an horizon style, the products of a particular district are easily identified by their local characteristics and are seldom found outside it.

The Central Andes

The central Andean region consists of the mountain belt of Peru and Bolivia, bounded on the west by the arid coastal plain of Peru where life is only possible in the river valleys, and on the east by the forests surrounding the headwaters of the Amazon. The highland region is itself very varied, consisting of bleak plateaux, high passes, snow-capped peaks, and comparatively sheltered valleys and basins. The irrigated valleys of the coast were separated by desert stretches which hindered free communication. The forests were little inhabited and do not concern us here.

SOUTH AMERICA

The central Andes were the scene of the highest development, not only of civilization in general, but also of the potter's art in South America. Here we find examples of the most advanced methods of manufacture and almost every decorative process used by South American potters. In many non-industrial communities pottery making is a craft at which any woman is an adept, but the elaboration of much central Andean pottery is such that it may have become the work of specialists at an early date, and, like some such specialists in other parts of the world, they may have been men. The degree of control attained in firing also suggests the early replacement of open fires by some sort of kiln.

Utilitarian pottery is first known about 1200 B.C. among rather humble people who lived by fishing and small-scale farming near the mouths of the north coast rivers. It consists of plain egg-shaped jars with rounded bottoms, which were at first used merely as containers and not for cooking. It is uncertain whether the coiling method of manufacture was used for these and later simple forms, or whether they were hand modelled.

About 800 B.C. appeared a more advanced people, who built elaborate temples and worshipped a cat god, probably the puma in origin, and they seem to have become the rulers of the early farmer-fishermen. Their rule is believed to have been based rather on religion than on force, and signs of their cat-worship are widely distributed in Peru. The sudden appearance of this complex culture, which is named Chavín or Cupisnique, shows that it must have developed elsewhere, though the place is at present unknown. The Chavín people introduced maize and other traits, including some very remarkable decorated pottery which was used exclusively for ceremonial purposes, notably for burial with the dead. It never forms more than a very small proportion of the potsherds found on dwelling sites, where the utilitarian forms continued with little change. The most striking feature of the majority of Cupisnique pots is the stirrup spout, which has a long history, since in one form or another it persists right up to the time of the Spanish Conquest. The Cupisnique examples are normally heavy and massive by comparison with later ones, and the mouth is slightly flanged, characteristics which are well seen in Plate 50. In three cases which have been studied by X-ray photography the arched portion was made in one piece, in contrast with some later examples which were built up from several. The body of the pot takes many forms, and is believed to have been made with the aid of moulds, which were themselves made of pottery. The objects represented include animals or their heads, fruits and vegetables, sea shells, and very rarely human figures or houses, moulded in the round or less commonly in low relief (1). A large class is roughly globular in outline with a flattened base, the surface being decorated with incised or punctate geometrical designs, some of which may be conventional representations of the fangs of the feline deity. The life forms are skilfully modelled but they do not reach the high degree of realism which was afterwards attained in this area, particularly in the Mochica pottery. The ware varies a good deal in quality, and is generally grey in colour. The temper is normally rather coarse, but in at least one of the three examples available for study in this country it is very fine. In these examples the colour is due rather to smudging with carbon in the fire than to chemical reduction, since it tends to be superficial, and the interior of the fabric may be red or reddish. All three are hard, one of them extremely so.

Various local developments followed and technical processes were improved, particularly in agriculture, which was increasingly based on irrigation, as well as in pottery, weaving and metal-working. Owing to the dry climate and the consequent preservation of perishable materials, most of our knowledge of this stage comes from the coast; it is known that weaving developed most quickly in the south parts of that area, and metal working, of gold, copper, silver and some of their alloys, in the north. The rarity of material evidence of cat-worship suggests that it was becoming obsolete. The chief advances in potting, at least in the north and central coastal areas, seem to have been a greater care in the preparation of the clay, together with the introduction of coarse brush painting. The result is seen in the prevalence of well-fired vessels, generally red in colour, which may have decoration in white or a more vivid red, used either to pick out modelled detail or to form simple geometrical designs. A common form of white painted decoration is a zone of inverted triangles, covered with dots, encircling the upper part of the body of the pot. Many of the vessels take the form of a simple jar, with a tall, narrow neck and strap handle, but the Cupisnique modelling tradition continues in the north coast, though life forms tend to be rather more conventional and the moulded shapes are often supplemented by appliqué details. The whistling jar makes its first appearance, in the form of a more or less globular vessel, sometimes carinated, with two vents connected by an arched bridge; one of these takes the form of a human figure combined with a small globular whistle, through which air must pass when water is poured in or out through the other, which is a spout.

A decorative process of considerable importance, which appeared a

---

(1) *Plate* 51.

little later, is negative painting, in which designs appear in the colour of the surface of the pot against a black background. This is comparable with the batik method of decorating cloth and is done by painting the designs in wax and then dipping the vessel in black pigment; the vessel is then fired and the wax melts, carrying away the black which overlies it, while the rest remains. The black ground may be rather thin and fugitive, and the name 'lost-colour ware' has been used for pottery decorated in this way, particularly for a much later variety found in Panamá. A notable early example of the process is found on the pottery of Recuay in the northern section of the Peruvian Andes. Here is found a great variety of vessel forms of white clay, with positive decoration in red and overall negative designs in black, which generally take the form of an angular stylized puma with a large head comb (1). Some vessels, such as bowls and jars, are simple in shape, but complex forms are also typical. These range from squat jars with a modelled head on the shoulder and a low neck surmounted by a wide, flange-like rim, to vessels representing scenes which may include buildings, men and llamas.

In the south coastal region, a most peculiar pottery style is found in connexion with the early occupation of the Paracas Peninsula known as Paracas Cavernas. The forms are very varied and include open bowls, globular jars with two spouts connected by a bridge, and modelled life forms. Many are decorated with incised lines enclosing areas of bright colour, yellow, green and red, with a predominantly black background, all apparently applied after firing since it flakes off when washed. The designs include feline faces with fangs, which suggest Cupisnique influence. Negative designs of simple character, normally consisting of groups of dots, are found on some pots. The jar, representing a deformed trophy head, shown in Plates 54, 55, from the Gothenburg Museum, is typical of the bizarre appearance of this ware. This Paracas Cavernas pottery foreshadows characteristics of south coast pottery which were to develop more strongly later; namely, the way of depicting life forms, which is generally inferior to that of the north coast, and the use of many colours, as opposed to two or at most three which were used in the north at the same time.

The acme of technological development seems to have been reached in the last few centuries B.C. or the beginning of the Christian era, when a considerable state, which we call Mochica, flourished in a group of north coastal valleys, centring in that of the Chicama river, while smaller groups of people, probably related to one another, lived in the south, in the Nazca valley and near the Paracas peninsula.

---

(1) *Plate* 52.

Both Mochica and Nazca peoples are well known for their pottery, and Paracas has yielded fine textiles. Meanwhile an important culture arose in the Highlands; it had a notable religious centre at Tiahuanaco, near Lake Titicaca in Bolivia, but its main focus of development is now believed to have been at Huari, in the central Andes. The remains found at Tiahuanaco include an enormous monolithic gateway, great flights of steps and impressive stone statues. This stage was marked, not only by a mastery of technical processes, but by the increasing prominence of fighting and war. Religious chiefs were also war chiefs.

In the north coast, the highest developments, both in technique and in artistry, are found in the ceremonial pottery of the Mochica Culture. The outstanding feature is modelling in the round or in low relief combined with brush painting in red and white, with the addition of a little black in the later stages when signs of degeneration begin to appear. The modelled forms were made in pottery moulds, and this frequently resulted in the production of near duplicates, though minor differences were generally introduced during the finishing process. The low relief decoration, which became commoner in later times, is usually described as pressed relief. The vessels take many forms, prominent among which is the globular or modelled jar with a flat base and a graceful stirrup spout, generally lighter in construction than the Cupisnique ones (1). Another common shape is a jar, often modelled to represent a human or animal body, or the head only, with the opening formed by a simple neck expanding slightly upwards. Graceful funnel-shaped bowls are also found, flaring widely out to an almost horizontal lip and standing on a bung foot, which may contain a pellet which rattles when moved. There are also ladle-like vessels with a constricted aperture and a slightly curved handle, which are known as dippers, or poppers, the latter name from a conjecture that the plain examples could have been used for roasting popcorn (2). Musical instruments were sometimes made of pottery, notably end-blown trumpets, straight, looped or made in the form of a conch shell, and rattles. Bowls and dippers, as well as stirrup-spouted and other jars which are not elaborately modelled, may be painted with scenes, some of them extremely complex (3).

The decoration of this pottery, painted or modelled or a combination of both, may be deliberately stylized; but it often attains a high degree of realism, and it forms an important source of information about the life and customs of the people. It gives us a vivid picture of

(1) *Plates* 53, 56, and *Colour Plate* A; (2) *Plates* 58, 59; (3) *Plates* 57, 60.

an elaborately organized state with many distinctions of both class and occupation, and glimpses of religion are afforded by richly clad figures of gods or demons, animal (1) or partly human, sometimes fighting with one another. Prominent among these is a human figure with feline tusks, perhaps a descendant of the feline god of earlier times. Some pots show scenes of ceremony, hunting or battle, others represent chiefs, priests, messengers (2), musicians, warriors or naked prisoners, who may retain elaborate headdresses to show their rank. Women are shown rather plainly clad, denoting a status generally inferior to that of the men. Some jars must be portraits (3), some show people with identifiable diseases or deliberate mutilations of limb or face, and some represent corpses or skeletons. Other representations include buildings and reed rafts with fishermen, while fruits, animals, birds (4), or abstract forms (5) are superbly modelled or painted on many jars. Whistling jars are frequent and often take the form of birds.

A vast number of Mochica pots have been removed from the cemeteries, chiefly by professional grave robbers, and have found their way into museums and private collections all over the world. So, in contrast with some of the earlier cultures, it is easy to see and study examples.

Pottery reached its highest development in the south coast in the Nazca Culture, probably at much the same time as the Mochica Culture flourished in the north, and certainly later than Paracas Cavernas. It is thin, well made, and polished, but modelling in the round is rare by comparison with the Mochica and when it occurs it generally takes the form of highly stylized human beings or trophy heads (6). Pressed relief is absent. The most characteristic form is a globular jar with two short tubular spouts connected by a flat bridge (7), but bowls (8) and beakers of various forms are common. Both the latter types have gently rounded bases, and the bowls may be shallow with straight, outsloping sides, or deep with concave sides. The beakers are similar, but the sides are vertical though they may be slightly waisted (9). Spheroidal bowls with the aperture less than the greatest diameter, flaring lip, and two loop handles on the shoulder, are also found. Human figure jars (10) generally have a single spout, connected to the back of the figure by a bridge. Nazca pottery is painted in up to eight colours on a background slip, the usual colours being black, white and various shades of red, yellow, brown, grey and violet, with the designs

---

(1) *Plate* 60; (2) *Plate* 57; (3) *Colour Plate* A; (4) *Plate* 61; (5) *Plate* 56; (6) *Plate* 62A; (7) *Plate* 62B, C; (8) *Plate* 63A; (9) *Colour Plate* D; (10) *Plate* 63B.

generally outlined in black. Most of the earlier pots have rather a sombre red background, but white grounds become common later. Designs fall into two main classes; the first consisting of recognizable though highly stylized life forms, such as birds, fish or fruit; and the second of themes inspired by religion or mythology, such as trophy heads or complex demons, among which is a centipede with a feline head or mask. Like the Mochica, Nazca pots are common in museums.

In the southern highlands the neighbourhood of Tiahuanaco has yielded a well-recognized pottery style which is believed to have been at its best at about the same time as the Nazca and Mochica on the coast. The commonest forms are a graceful, hollow-sided beaker (1) and various forms of vase or bottle. Open bowls with a slight constriction halfway up the wall also occur (2); and there are characteristic animal vessels, in the form of a shallow bowl with a boldly modelled head, generally of a puma with a flangelike collar, on one side and a tail on the other. As in the neighbouring south coast, the vessels are painted in polychrome. In the best period, sometimes called the Classic, the ground is always a red slip, and the overlying colours—yellow, brown or grey, outlined by black or white—though originally bright, may weather rather faint and indistinct. The designs are either conventional pumas or condors, or are geometrical; for example, triangles or a combination expressively called the step-fret. The animals and birds are shown in profile and their eyes are frequently divided vertically—'party' as the heralds say—into black and white halves. The pumas have a round knob balanced, like a lump of sugar, on the end of the nose (3).

In the same neighbourhood, perhaps a little earlier, a related though distinct style is found at Pucára, some distance north of the lake. Little is known of the shapes of the pots since the excavation of the site has not yet been fully published, but open bowls of various types seem to be frequent, including a shallow variety with a ring base. The decoration of the finer types is characteristic; they have a buff or reddish buff slip, over which are areas of red and black paint outlined by lines engraved when the clay was nearly dry. Designs include step-frets and similar geometrical forms, and human and feline heads. Painted puma heads in low relief are also found, and the eyes of these and of the painted and engraved human and animal heads are 'party' like those at Tiahuanaco, but in this case black and buff. Mica was commonly used as a tempering material.

It has already been pointed out that the Mochica Nazca and Classic Tiahuanaco styles mark the highest development of pottery

---

(1) *Plate* 64; (2) *Plate* 65; (3) *Plate* 65.

D. *Polychrome beaker. Nazca culture, Peru, probably 7th century* A.D. *Height* $6\frac{7}{8}$ *in.*
British Museum
(*See p.* 35)

in their respective areas, but they are far from the end of the story. Many later potters equalled them in technical skill, but their products were generally inferior in artistic quality, and sometimes in paste and decorative technique.

At the end of Mochica and Nazca times, clashes between the various regions seem to have led up to the conquest of most of the coast by the bearers of the Huari or Tiahuanaco culture, whose art style is found over a wide area on coastal pottery and textiles. This conquest probably took place towards the end of the first millennium A.D. It is marked by the introduction of a widespread pottery style known as Coast Tiahuanaco or Epigonal, but local styles are still found though the old ones had disappeared. The Coast Tiahuanaco style is found throughout the coast except in the extreme north, and from the coast it seems to have spread into the northern highlands. It differs from the pottery found at Tiahuanaco itself but is decorated with Tiahuanaco motifs derived both from pottery and from stone carvings; they include pumas and condors which may have party eyes, running figures with bird masks shown in profile, and a human figure shown full face carrying staves in both hands, or a head alone. The designs are brightly painted in polychrome in the southern tradition, with black, white, grey and yellow on a red slip and are sometimes divided into panels by bands of chevrons. The most usual pottery shapes are spheroidal vessels with two tapering spouts connected by a flat bridge (1), beakers and cups (2), and jars with a high neck which may have a face painted, flat or in relief, on it. Large painted jars in the form of llamas, some of them about four feet high, opening through a collar in the middle of the back, were found in fragments at Pacheco in the Nazca Valley, and, after repair, are among the most remarkable exhibits in the National Museum at Lima. From the same site come powerfully modelled human heads, covered with rather friable dark crimson paint, except for the great staring white eyes with dark pupils. They probably formed part of large jars. A local characteristic of the north coast is blackware decorated with pressed relief, and two-colour negative ware survives in modified form in the north highlands.

After a time, the highland influence on the coast decayed, and the Tiahuanaco motifs on pottery tended to break down into geometrical forms which were painted in black, white and red. Among the shapes common over much of the coast are globular jars with flaring collars and a pair of loop handles, and flaring-sided beakers. Finally three states emerged on the coast, in the north, centre and south, the most important being the northern one, the Chimu, which covered roughly

(1) *Plate* 66B; (2) *Plate* 66A.

the same region as the Mochica and can be considered its successor. Each of the areas occupied by these states has its characteristic pottery style, but that of the Chimu alone has appreciable traits in common with its pre-Tiahuanaco predecessor, thus testifying to the strength of the tradition in the north. This stage is marked by the rise, for the first time, of great cities, of which the best example is Chan-Chan, the Chimu capital, whose ruins can still be seen near Trujillo. The date of the beginning of these states is not known, but they flourished until overcome by the Incas in the fifteenth century.

The pottery style of the central state is a simplification of the black, white, red style by the elimination of the red colour and sometimes even the black. The ware is thin and porous, dull red or cream in colour with a creamy white slip, and takes the form of egg-shaped jars with a collar and a pair of loop handles, similar jars with a human face on the collar and skimpy limbs in relief (1), and spheroidal bowls. The main focus of the style was the Chancay Valley and it is known as the Chancay Black-on-White, or White, style. In both material and decoration, it gives an impression of degeneracy. The ceramics of the neighbourhood of Ica are characteristic of the southern state. They are of hard, burnished, buff, orange, or dull red ware, decorated with textile-derived patterns in black, white and red, either geometrical designs or small birds or fish. The commonest forms are globular jars with constricted necks and flaring collars, and bowls of various forms with angular outlines and solid, chamfered rims (2). The pottery of the important Chimu State in the north is nearly always of a single colour, either grey to black or red, and polished, the black being produced by firing in a reducing atmosphere combined with smoking. Painted vases are rare, and are generally decorated in red on a white slip. The modelling tradition of the Mochica was revived by the Chimu, but though a wide variety of shapes was produced they are artistically much inferior to those of the older period. Pressed relief was also commonly employed for decoration. The vessels take many forms, prominent among which is another Mochica survival, the stirrup spout, but now it is generally square in section and has a little animal, such as a monkey, modelled at the junction of the stirrup and the spout (3). Other common forms are the double vase, which may be a whistler, and a flask, globular or modelled in some life form, with a flaring neck. Some vessels, particularly the double ones, have a spout connected to a modelled figure by a bridge, a form derived from the Huari expansion. In addition there are many miscellaneous modelled forms, including animal heads, human limbs, and

---

(1) *Plate* 67; (2) *Plate* 68A; (3) *Plate* 68B.

fishermen on rafts (1). Generally speaking, the wares of this period, particularly in the north and centre, with their reduced number of colours and inartistic modelling, give an impression of mass production, and a preoccupation with quantity rather than quality.

The Incas were originally a small tribe, which settled in a pleasant highland valley at Cuzco about A.D. 1200. After fighting various small wars, they narrowly escaped conquest by a neighbouring group of tribes early in the fifteenth century. Having overcome these enemies, they allied themselves with them and started on a career of conquest and expansion, which carried them, in a brief ninety years, along the Andes to the north of Ecuador, over the whole Peruvian coast, southwards through Bolivia to N.W. Argentina and along the coast into Chile. Although it was sometimes necessary to fight, much of this area including the great Chimu state was absorbed by threats and diplomacy. This is not the place to describe the way in which this great Empire was organized and consolidated, and it must suffice to say that there is plenty of archaeological evidence for its extent, in the shape of Inca types of masonry and Inca pottery forms. The high degree of centralization achieved must be held largely responsible for the rapid conquest of the Empire by a handful of Spaniards, once they had captured the Emperor, the heart of the whole system.

The finest pottery of the Incas belongs to the period of their expansion in the fifteenth century. There are few shapes and these are highly characteristic. Prominent among them is that now named after the Greek aryballus (2). This was originally a water-jar made to be carried on the back by means of a rope passing through the handles and over the nubbin (in the form of a conventionalized animal head) at the base of the neck; but it is found in all sizes down to miniatures only a few inches high. Plates, with a bird-head handle and a pair of small projections representing the tail on the opposite side, are another very common type (3), and jars and flat-based bowls with broad strap handles (4) are also very frequent. A peculiar type of drinking vessel, called in the Inca language *paccha*, sometimes incorporates an aryballus (5). The ware is red in colour, well made and polished, and is generally painted in polychrome. The commonest colours are red, white and black; but yellow and orange are sometimes added, particularly in pottery made in the Titicaca area. The decoration is generally geometrical in character, for example, bands of hatched diamonds (6) or triangles; but there is one common form which seems to be a stylized plant (7); and small conventionalized butterflies, bees

---

(1) *Plate* 68B; (2) *Plate* 69; (3) *Plate* 70A; (4) *Plate* 70B; (5) *Plate* 71; (6) *Plate* 69; (7) *Plate* 71.

or llamas are sometimes represented. As the Inca Empire grew, the standard pottery forms were carried far and wide, and were made in the local wares. In Chile, for example, we find plates with bird-head handles, painted in a provincial style; and the aryballus in black ware with pressed relief ornament is frequent in the Chimu area. Inca shapes also influenced local forms, producing hybrids like the late Chimu whistling vessel consisting of two joined globular jars, with tall necks which are clearly inspired by the aryballus. With the Spanish conquest in the sixteenth century our period comes to an end, but this form of whistling jar at least survived and a number of examples have been found covered with a European green glaze.

Ecuador and Colombia

Ecuador, like Peru, consists of three main zones, the coast, the highlands and the Amazon forests, but its pre-Inca civilizations show far closer relationships with Colombia and parts of central America than with Peru. Much of the material evidence for this comes from pottery, which shows few specific resemblances to Peruvian types, though most of the processes of manufacture and decoration are common to both areas. Within Ecuador, highland ceramics differ considerably from those of the coast.

The highland zone consists of a series of intermont basins lying in a north-south line, separated by high passes and flanked by snow-capped volcanoes. The Incas conquered this area in the fifteenth century, and it is known that it was occupied at this time by six tribes, each of them confined to one or exceptionally two basins, a distribution which is confirmed by the archaeology insofar as it is known. An eighteenth century historian, Father Juan de Velasco, wrote a *History of the Kingdom of Quito* in which he gave an account of the Caras, a tribe which lived in the north of the area, claiming that they had built up a kingdom extending over much of the highlands. The modern view is that this is much exaggerated, though it is likely that they formed some kind of confederation with the two tribes to the south of them at the time of the Inca conquest, and that their ruling family had intermarried with that of the Puruhá, the southernmost of the three. To the south of this group, occupying the pleasant basin of Cuenca and adjacent areas in the provinces of Azuay and Cañar, were the Cañaris, whose land was conquered and settled by the Incas after bitter resistance, before the Caras and their associates were attacked. Large parts of the highland area have not been studied and it is not possible to give a chronological account of it, or, with rare exceptions, to assign pottery styles to particular periods. The most that can be done here is to notice a few of the more characteristic types.

There is a great variety of monochrome vessels, generally of some sort of polished red ware, and among these, bowls of various kinds are conspicuous. A common type is the tripod bowl, a form which is scarcely ever found in Peru, except in a restricted area in the northern highlands. The vessels depend for their decorative effect, if any, on complexity of outline (1), the addition of small modelled details or incision. One interesting type, mainly found in the north, is a bowl modelled to represent an animal lying on its back with the opening in its stomach (2). Generally, however, modelling, particularly that of the human figure, is very crude. Among painted wares, a common type has simple red linear designs on a buff slip (3), but the most notable style is based on the same process as that of Recuay in Peru, namely simple red designs (for example bands, quadrants or discs) on a buff slip with overall negative decoration in black.[1] This style, which has been named Tuncahuán, is best developed in the province of Carchi in the extreme north and in the adjacent part of Colombia, but a closely similar one is found, probably at a later date, in a detached area further south, chiefly in the province of Chimborazo, the region occupied by the Puruhá tribe. In the northern area, the vessels take two principal forms, namely large pear-shaped jars with a tall, flaring neck, and open bowls with straight sides sloping outwards at about 45° on a low ring base (4). The figure modelling of Recuay is lacking, and the style is believed to be very much later in date than Recuay. The negative decoration on the jars and some bowls is geometrical, but the interiors of some bowls have a pair of stylized monkeys shown in outline and symmetrically arranged (4). The combination of some of the geometrical designs with the underlying red is very attractive. The vessels in the southern area are mainly bowls with curved sides, slightly constricted at the mouth, and the ring bases, where present, are tall and flare downwards. The decoration is geometrical or curvilinear. The province of Cañar, between Azuay and Chimborazo, is distinguished by a long-lived red-on-buff style, which is probably to be ascribed to the Cañaris since it lasted into Inca times, though the prevalence of very different types in Azuay, also part of their territory, in late prehistoric times is one of the many unresolved puzzles of Ecuadorean archaeology. The earlier examples of red-on-buff pottery

[1] In the original description of this ware it is stated that the red was applied over the black negative paint, but in the examples available for examination there is no doubt that the red was put on first, as at Recuay and on similar wares in Colombia and Panama. Vessels of this style are well illustrated in colour in Verneau and Rivet, *Ethnographie Ancienne de l'Equateur*, Vol. 2, Paris, 1922.

---

(1) *Plate* 73A; (2) *Plate* 72A; (3) *Plate* 73B; (4) *Plate* 72B.

may be very fine in quality, but a very coarse type appeared later and eventually predominated. The normal vessel form is the globular jar with a low, flaring rim, and the painted designs are generally very simple, such as bands encircling the body and rim. The coarse forms include large cylindrical vessels 10 to 30 cm. high closed at one end by a concave septum with a hole in the middle, which may have been seats or drums. Another Cañar type is a large jar, shaped like the Tuncahuán one of Carchi, but decorated with geometrical figures in thick white paint on a chocolate slip (1).

The coastal plain is much wider than the corresponding zone in Peru, and much of the interior and north fall into the tropical forest region. Only the south-west, just north of the Gulf of Guayaquil, approaches the Peruvian coast in aridity. Our knowledge of the ancient civilizations is as patchy here as it is in the highlands, and large areas have not been studied. In the north is the Province of Esmeraldas, which is known for a multitude of highly varied mould-made figurines, believed to have been inspired by central American prototypes, though the buff, sandy ware is characteristic of the area and shows that they were locally made. As far as our present knowledge goes, the culture associated with them occupied the area for a long period. Further south, just north of the Gulf of Guayaquil, remains of a series of cultures have been found, and the pottery of each is so different from the others that it is likely that at least three distinct peoples occupied the area successively. There is some reason to believe that the same happened in the Province of Manabí to the north of this area, between it and Esmeraldas. The Incas invaded Manabí from the highlands, but left no traces of their presence in the more southerly district, except on the Island of Puná in the Guayas estuary. Only two of the successive cultures call for mention on account of their pottery, the Guangala, which is probably second in point of age, and the final one, the Manteño. The Guangala includes a number of interesting pottery types of which the finest, which is decorated in black and red on a yellow ground, is so similar in execution to Nicoya Polychrome ware as to suggest that the makers brought the style direct by sea from Costa Rica. Hollow figurines containing whistles, which are similar to one variety of the Esmeraldas figurines but are made of fine polished red ware of local origin, are an important link with Esmeraldas (2). A type, known only from incomplete examples, and which seems to be unique, is a shallow open red ware bowl, supported on five or six solid pointed feet, generally bearing applied decorations representing a stylized human face. Tripods are common in America, and tetrapods

(1) *Plate* 74; (2) *Plate* 76.

are not lacking, but this seems to be the only instance of vessels with more than four feet.

The latest culture, the Manteño, covers the whole coast to the south of the Province of Esmeraldas, and is associated with a number of related tribes whose names were recorded by Spanish chroniclers. The pottery is all of a single colour and is generally grey, sometimes buff. Ornament is produced by engraving, by application of modelled detail, or by burnishing part of the surface, making it appear darker than the surrounding matt surface. The applied detail generally consists of human or animal faces on the collars of jars, and the burnished ornament of lines, spirals, bands and stylized human limbs. The fine face-jar illustrated shows arms and possibly garments represented in this way (1). Besides face-jars, which are frequent, various forms of bowl are commonly found, and the same ware was used to make solid figurines in moulds, and spindle whorls which bear striking champlevé designs, including pelicans, owls and monkeys. This pottery is very different from the Chimu blackware, but its dull colour and lack of painted decoration show that a similar taste for drabness affected both north-west Peru and south-west Ecuador in late prehistoric times.

Most of the known ancient cultures of Colombia fall within the highland zone, which is much broader and more complex than those of Ecuador and Peru, and consists of no fewer than four mountain chains running from north to south, with deep valleys and some high basins between them. Nine separate archaeological regions have been distinguished, but there are large unstudied areas separating them, and little is known of their mutual relations and next to nothing of their chronology. The country must have been inhabited by a number of small tribes, but in one region only was there any sign of a larger organization. Round the modern towns of Bogotá and Tunja, in the Eastern Cordillera, are some extensive high basins in which dwelt the Chibchas, a group of related tribes which formed a loose confederation at the time of the arrival of the Spaniards; but the confederation showed few signs of developing further, since the tribes were constantly fighting among themselves. The pottery of the Chibchas is not distinguished by a high degree of artistry. The paste is white or buff, coarsely tempered, rough or imperfectly polished, and generally unpainted but sometimes painted red. Decoration is frequently incised or stamped, rows of dots in circles being very common; and highly stylized human figures with applied details often form part or the whole of vessels. The modelling is sometimes exceedingly crude (2).

---

(1) *Plate* 75; (2) *Plate* 77.

The most common vessel forms are globular jars, with collars which may bear modelled faces, and pedestal bowls.

The pottery of only one other area of Colombia requires mention here, namely the Quimbaya zone which lies in and around the central part of the Cauca valley, a region also distinguished for the excellence of its gold work. It is generally far better in quality than the Chibcha wares; the tempering material is finer, the decorated vessels are usually slipped, and there is considerable variety in type, though this may be partly due to age differences. Negative-painted ware is highly characteristic, and is either in two colours, black on red, or in three, black on white and red (1). The latter type resembles very closely the Tuncahuán style of North Ecuador and the extreme south of Colombia on one hand, and the 'lost colour' ware of Chiriquí in Panama on the other. Since the Panamanian ware appears to have been made until shortly before the arrival of the Europeans, and the three-colour negative of Recuay is very old, it is possible that this technique diffused slowly northwards from Peru to the Isthmus. The shapes include bowls of various forms; simple, angular and pedestalled jars and jugs; and very poorly modelled human-figure jars, which may have metal nose rings. Another technique, which seems to be peculiar to this area, is known as champlevé, though chip-carved is perhaps more expressive, since the surface, which may or may not be slipped, is decorated by the removal of deep triangular or quadrangular chips grouped in areas of geometrical shapes. A common form is a rounded bowl, less than a hemisphere, surmounted by a narrow, sharply-inturned rim (2). A third distinct style is known as brown-incised, and is made of brown-slipped ware with shallow incisions, generally in the form of vertical bands of herring-bone ornament. The usual form is a rather thick-walled, flat-bottomed beaker, with vertical sides, either straight or bowing out in the lower part, and a deep groove just below the lip. Finally there are two types of red and white painted ware, which resemble Peruvian forms in a general way; the double jar, in which a modelled bird, animal or human figure is connected to a plain jar by a tube and bridge; and the double-spouted jar. Owing to their local characteristics and their geographical isolation, it is extremely doubtful if these jars indicate any direct Peruvian influence.

North-West Argentina and Northern Chile

North-west Argentina, the highland zone between the Bolivian border and the Province of San Juan just north of Mendoza, is an area

(1) *Plate* 78; (2) *Plate* 79B.

where developments were distinct from those of the central Andean region, and there is good reason to group a large part of northern Chile with it. Both regions were overrun by the Inca late in the fifteenth century, and incorporated in the Empire.

Of the indigenous pottery styles, the best are associated with the name of the Diaguite, a tribe or group of tribes speaking a common language, who inhabited a large part of both areas when the Spaniards arrived. There are a number of different styles and they must cover a considerable period of time. But little stratigraphical excavation has been done, and it is by no means certain that the Diaguite made all the pottery they are credited with, though they are reliably connected with a distinctive group of styles in Chile.

Chilean Diaguite pottery persisted into Inca times but the age of its first manufacture is unknown. There are two main styles whose mutual relationship is still obscure. The first consists of rather thick vessels, decorated in red, white and a colour which is more often grey than black. Geometrical motifs, particularly step-frets and zigzags, are always used, but they may be interrupted by a highly-conventionalized face, with some details roughly indicated in relief. The commonest form is a bowl with rounded base and vertical sides, which are straight or slightly waisted, the decoration being confined to the exterior. Other types include oval-bodied jars with the opening set asymmetrically to form either a duck pot (1) or a head and spout jar, a form doubtless derived from southern Peru. Plain brown utilitarian duck pots, similar to those of the Anasazi of the southwest of the United States with the addition of a handle, are also found. The second principal decorated style consists mainly of round-bottomed bowls with flaring sides, thinner and lighter than the other. They are decorated in the same three colours, but the black has not the tendency to fade to grey which is so marked a feature of the first style. Most of the painted decoration consists of similar geometrical motifs on the outside; but four small animals, symmetrically disposed, may be painted in black on the white-slipped interior, in a style reminiscent of Cuzco Inca work.

In north-west Argentina the most striking and well-known pottery type is the Santa Maria urn, a large vessel which commonly has a small flattened or impressed base, an ovoid body to which are attached two strap handles (2), applied so that the opening is vertical, and a high flaring neck. The urns are decorated in black on a yellow or white slip and the designs are very complex, but in general seem to represent a highly stylized human figure clad in elaborate textiles.

---

(1) *Plate* 79A; (2) *Plate* 80.

The Santa Maria urn comes from the central part of the area, while another type, the Belen urn, is believed to have been roughly contemporary with it in the south. This is similar in general form but much squatter, and it may have a pair of miniature men or animals applied to the body above the handles. The painted decoration is typically black on red, and much simpler than the typical Santa Maria examples. Painted motifs, like the snakes in Plate 80, may be outlined by wide grooves. These urns are believed to be considerably pre-Inca in date, and to have been preceded in both areas by other pottery types, including black ware with incised decoration.

Here, as in so much of western South America, the Inca conquest is attested by the presence of Inca polychrome pottery and in some parts by local modified Inca forms.

BIBLIOGRAPHY

THE SOUTHWEST OF THE UNITED STATES

H. M. WORMINGTON, *Prehistoric Indians of the Southwest.* Denver Museum of Natural History, Denver, Colorado. Popular Series No. 7, 2nd Edition, 1951.

MEXICO

G. VAILLANT, 'Excavations at Zacatenco.' 'Excavations at El Arbolillo.' 'Excavations at Gualupita.' 'Early Cultures of the Valley of Mexico.' *Anthropological Papers of the America Museum of Natural History*. New York, 1930–6.

S. LINNÉ, *Archaeological Researches at Teotihuacan, Mexico.* The Ethnographical Museum of Sweden, Publication No. 1, Stockholm, 1934.

Zapotecan Antiquities. The Ethnographical Museum of Sweden, Publication No. 4 (N.S.), Stockholm, 1938.

PHILIP DRUKER, *La Venta, Tabasco, A Study of Olmec Ceramics and Art.* Bureau of American Ethnology, Washington, 1952.

W. JIMÉNEZ MORENO, *Introducción á la Guia arqueológica de Tula.* Mexico, 1947.

F. BOAS AND M. GAMIO, 'Estudio de la Ceramica Azteca,' *Album de collectiones Arqueologicas.* Publicationes de la Escuela internacional de Arqueologia y Etnologia Americanas, Mexico, 1921.

D. BRAND, 'The distribution of Pottery Types in Northwestern Mexico,' *American Anthropologist*, Vol. 37. 1935

ANNA O. SHEPARD, *Plumbate, A mesoamerican Trade Ware.* Carnegie Institution of Washington, Publication No. 573, Washington, 1948.

MIGUEL COVARRUBIAS, *Mexico South.* London (Cassel & Co.), 1948.

ANCIENT AMERICAN POTTERY

THE MAYA

SYLVANUS G. MORLEY, *The Ancient Maya*. Stanford, 1946.

A. LEDYARD SMITH, *Uaxactun, Guatemala: Excavations of* 1931–7. Carnegie Institution of Washington, Publication No. 588, Washington, 1950.

JOHN M. LONGYEAR III, *Copan Ceramics*. Carnegie Institution of Washington, Publication No. 597, Washington, 1952.

J. E. S. THOMPSON, *Excavations at San Jose, British Honduras*. Carnegie Institution of Washington, Publication No. 506, Washington, 1939.

A. V. KIDDER, J. D. JENNINGS AND E. M. SHOOK, *Excavations at Kaminaljuyu, Guatemala*. Carnegie Institution of Washington, Publication No. 561, Washington, 1946.

SOUTHERN CENTRAL AMERICA

S. K. LOTHROP, *Pottery of Nicaragua and Costa Rica*. Museum of The American Indian, Hege Foundation, Contribution No. 8, New York, 1926.

Coclé, Part II. Memoirs of The Peabody Museum of Archaeology and Ethnology, Harvard, Vol. VIII. Cambridge, Mass., 1942.

Archaeology of Southern Veraguas, Panama. Cambridge, Massachusetts, 1950.

G. G. MCCURDY, *A Study of Chiriquian Antiquities*. Yale University Press, New Haven, Conn., 1911.

COLOMBIA, ECUADOR, PERU AND CHILE

Handbook of South American Indians, Vol. 2. Smithsonian Institution, Bureau of American Ethnology, Bulletin 143, 1946.

W. C. BENNETT AND J. B. BIRD, *Andean Culture History*. American Museum of Natural History, Handbook Series No. 15, 1949.

JUNIUS BIRD, 'Radiocarbon Dating,' *American Antiquity*, Vol. XVII, No. 1, Part 2, July 1951.

G. H. S. BUSHNELL, *The Archaeology of the Santa Elena Peninsula in South-West Ecuador*. Cambridge University Press, 1951.

HEINRICH UBBELOHDE-DOERING, *The Art of Ancient Peru*. London, Zwemmer, 1952.

INDEX

INDEX

1. *Corrugated cooking pot. Developmental or Great Pueblo period. Probably from Zuñi Creek, New Mexico. Ht. 6 in. Cambridge University Museum of Archaeology and Ethnology*
(See p. 4)

2A. *Black-on-white bird jar. Developmental to Great Pueblo period. Probably from Zuñi Creek, New Mexico. Ht.* $6\frac{1}{2}$ *in. Cambridge University Museum of Archaeology and Ethnology.* (*See p.* 5)

2B. *Seed jar. Developmental Pueblo period. Mesa Redonda, Arizona. Ht.* $5\frac{1}{2}$ *in. Cambridge University Museum of Archaeology and Ethnology.* (*See p.* 5)

3A. *Black-on-white jar or pitcher. Developmental to Great Pueblo period. Mesa Redonda, Arizona. Ht.* $6\frac{1}{2}$ *in.*
Cambridge University Museum of Archaeology and Ethnology
(*See p.* 5)

3B. *Black-on-white ladle. Developmental Pueblo period. Probably from Zuñi Creek, New Mexico. Max. diam.* 5 *in.*
Cambridge University Museum of Archaeology and Ethnology
(*See p.* 5)

4A. *Black-on-white jar or pitcher. Great Pueblo period.*
Bought at Zuñi, New Mexico. Ht. 8 in.
Cambridge University Museum of Archaeology and Ethnology. (*See p.* 5)
4B. *Two black-on-white jars or pitchers of Tularosa ware. Great*
Pueblo period. Larger vessel about $6\frac{1}{2}$ *in. high.*
Denver Museum of Natural History, Colorado. (*See p.* 5)

5A. *Black-on-red bowl. Developmental to Great Pueblo period. St. John's, Arizona. Diam.* $8\frac{1}{2}$ *in. Cambridge University Museum of Archaeology and Ethnology.* (*See p.* 6)

5B. *Black-on-white bowl showing contrast of hatched and black areas, and dotted rim. Great Pueblo period. Mesa Verde, Colorado. Diam.* $10\frac{1}{4}$ *in. British Museum.* (*See p.* 5)

6A. *Black and white on red bowl. Regressive Pueblo period.*
Homolobi, Arizona. Ht. $3\frac{1}{2}$ *in.*
Cambridge University Museum of Archaeology and Ethnology. (*See p.* 6)
6B. *Salado-ware olla, red below, black-on-white above.*
Regressive Pueblo period. Kechipaun, near Zuñi, New Mexico. Diam. 12 *in.*
Cambridge University Museum of Archaeology and Ethnology. (*See p.* 6.)

7A. *Duck pot. Regressive Pueblo period. Kechipaun, near Zuñi, New Mexico. Length 9 in.*
Cambridge University Museum of Archaeology and Ethnology. (*See p.* 6)
7B. *Red-on-yellow olla. Regressive Pueblo period. Kechipaun, near Zuñi, New Mexico. Diam.* 10 *in.*
Cambridge University Museum of Archaeology and Ethnology. (*See p.* 7)

8A. *Polychrome olla (black and red on yellow). Regressive Pueblo period. Kechipaun, near Zuñi, New Mexico. Max. diam.* $10\frac{1}{2}$ *in. Cambridge University Museum of Archaeology and Ethnology.* (*See p.* 7).

8B. *Water jar decorated with conventionalized feathers, in red and white matt paint and dark green glaze. (Late period) Regressive Pueblo period. Kechipaun, near Zuñi, New Mexico. Diam.* 14 *in. Cambridge University Museum of Archaeology and Ethnology.* (*See p.* 7).

9 *Large jar of Sacaton red-on-buff ware. Hohokam Sedentary period. From Snaketown, Arizona. Diam. 24 in. Arizona State Museum*
(*See p.* 8)

10A. *Black and red on buff olla. Chihuahua, Mexico. Ht.* $6\frac{1}{2}$ *in.*
Cambridge University Museum of Archaeology and Ethnology. (*See p.* 9)
10B. '*Mimbres black-on-white' bowl* (*actually brown-on-white*).
Mimbres Valley, New Mexico. Diam. 10 *in.*
Cambridge University Museum of Archaeology and Ethnology. (*See p.* 9)

11A, B. *Figurines of the formative period. Ht.* (A) $2\frac{1}{4}$ *in.* (B) $3\frac{1}{2}$ *in. British Museum.* (*See p.* 12)

11C. *Corrugated bowl with basal angle. Probably from Tlatilco. Diam.* $5\frac{1}{2}$ *in. British Museum*

(*See p.* 12)

12. *Blackware vase in the form of a fish. From Tlatilco, formative period. Ht. $5\frac{1}{8}$ in.*
Museo Nacional de Antropología, Mexico
(*See p.* 13)

13. *Black-ware vase with cross-hatched ornament. From Tlatilco, formative period. Ht.* $8\frac{1}{4}$ *in. Museo Nacional de Antropología, Mexico*
(See p. 13)

14. *Wide-mouthed vase with scraped ornament. From Teotihuacán, III period. Ht.* $5\frac{3}{5}$ *in. British Museum*
(*See p.* 15)

15. *Effigy vase modelled in the form of Tlaloc, the rain god. Teotihuacán II period. Ht. 7⅝ in. British Museum*

(*See p.* 15)

16. *Wide-mouthed vase with cloisonné ornament. From Teotihuacán, II or III period. Ht 12 in. Museo Nacional de Antropología, Mexico*
(*See p.* 15)

17A, C. *Pottery figurines from Teotihuacán.* (A) *IV period*
(C) *II period. British Museum.* (*See p.* 15)
17B. *Florero. Teotihuacán, II period.*
Ht. $4\frac{7}{10}$ *in. British Museum.* (*See p.* 15)
17D. *Cylindrical tripod vase with carved zoomorphic ornament.*
Teotihuacán, III period, Ht. $5\frac{1}{8}$ *in.*
Museo Nacional de Antropología, Mexico. (*See p.* 15)

18A. *Polychrome vase with geometrical ornament. Maya, classic period, probably from the Ulua valley. Ht.* $5\frac{1}{4}$ *in. British Museum*
(*See p.* 17)

18B. *Polychrome bowl with nubbin feet and conventionalized glyphs. From Pusilha, British Honduras. Maya, Classic period. Diam.* $9\frac{7}{10}$ *in. British Museum*
(*See p.* 17)

19A. *Polychrome basal flanged bowl with ring base. Maya, classic period. Diam.* $13\frac{1}{5}$ *in. British Museum*
(*See p.* 17)

19B. *Polychrome plate with fish ornament. Maya, classic period, from British Honduras. Diam.* $12\frac{9}{10}$ *in. British Museum*
(*See p.* 17)

20. *Bowl with carved ornament. Maya, classic period, from the Alta Vera Paz district, Guatemala. Ht.* 5$\frac{3}{10}$ *in. British Museum*
(*See p.* 18)

21. *Polychrome cylindrical vase. Maya, late classic period, from Nebaj, Guatemala. Ht. 6½ in. British Museum*
(See p. 18)

22. *Spherical bowl with long spout and handle. Probably Monte Albán II period. Ht. 13 in. Collection of Sr Miguel Covarrubias*
(*See p.* 18)

23. *Incised tripod vase with large mammiform feet.*
Monte Albán I or II period. Ht. 9$\frac{13}{16}$ *in.*
Museo Nacional de Antropología, Mexico
(*See p.* 18)

24. *Funerary urn, representing the bat god. Monte Albán, III period. Ht.* 16 *in. British Museum*
(*See p.* 18)

25. *Funerary urn, probably representing the rain God Cocijo.*
Ht. 17½ *in. British Museum*
(*See p.* 18)

26. *Florero with carved ornament, grey with red paint in carved portions. Cerro de las Mesas, classic period. Ht. 7⅞ in. Museo Nacional de Antropología, Mexico*

(*See p.* 19)

27. *Pottery figurine, woman and child. Tarascan culture.*
Ht. 6$\frac{1}{10}$ *in. British Museum*
(*See p.* 19)

28. *Effigy vase in the form of a Mexican hairless dog. Colima.*
Ht. 12$\frac{1}{5}$ *in. British Museum*
(*See p.* 20)

29A. *Figurine with appliqué ornament. Chupícuaro. Ht.* 4 *in. Cambridge University Museum of Archaeology and Ethnology*
(*See p.* 20)

29B. *Polychrome bowl. Chupícuaro. Ht.* 6 *in. Cambridge University Museum of Archaeology and Ethnology*
(*See p.* 20)

30. *White and red tripod bowl. Chupícuaro. Ht.* $12\frac{5}{8}$ *in.*
Collection of Sr Fernando Gamboa, Mexico
(*See p.* 20)

31A. *Orange bowl, with red ornament.*
Mazápan culture. Diam. $7\frac{1}{2}$ *in.*
Cambridge University Museum of Archaeology and Ethnology
(See p. 21)

31B. *Maroon and white tripod bowl. Matlatzinca. Ht.* $6\frac{2}{5}$ *in.*
British Museum. *(See p.* 21)

32. *Plumbate-ware vase with cascable feet. Isla de los Sacrificios. Post-classic. Ht. 8½ in. British Museum*

(See p. 22)

35A. *Black-on-orange ware spindle bowl. Aztec II period.*
Diam. $2\frac{7}{10}$ *in. British Museum*
(*See p.* 24)
35B. *Black-on-orange ware bowl. Aztec II period.*
Diam. $7\frac{2}{5}$ *in. British Museum*
(*See p.* 24)

36A. *Bowl with red ornament in the form of crossed bones and skulls in red on white. Aztec IV period. Diam.* $6\frac{11}{16}$ *in.*
Museo Nacional de Antropología, Mexico. (*See p.* 24)
36B. *Biconical pulque cup. Aztec III period. Ht.* $5\frac{3}{5}$ *in.*
British Museum. (*See p.* 24)

37A. *Bowl with black ornament on red. Aztec IV period. Diam.* $4\frac{1}{2}$ *in. Cambridge University Museum of Archaeology and Ethnology.* (*See p.* 24)
37B. *Pulque cup with incised and black painted ornament on red. Aztec III or IV period. Ht.* $6\frac{3}{10}$ *in. British Museum.* (*See p.* 24)

38. *Polychrome tripod chocolate vase. Mixteca Puebla culture.*
Ht. $6\frac{11}{16}$ *in. Museo Nacional de Antropología, Mexico*

(*See p.* 24)

39. *Polychrome ewer. Mixteca Puebla culture. Ht.* $6\frac{5}{16}$ *in.*
Museo Nacional de Antropología, Mexico
(*See p. 24*)

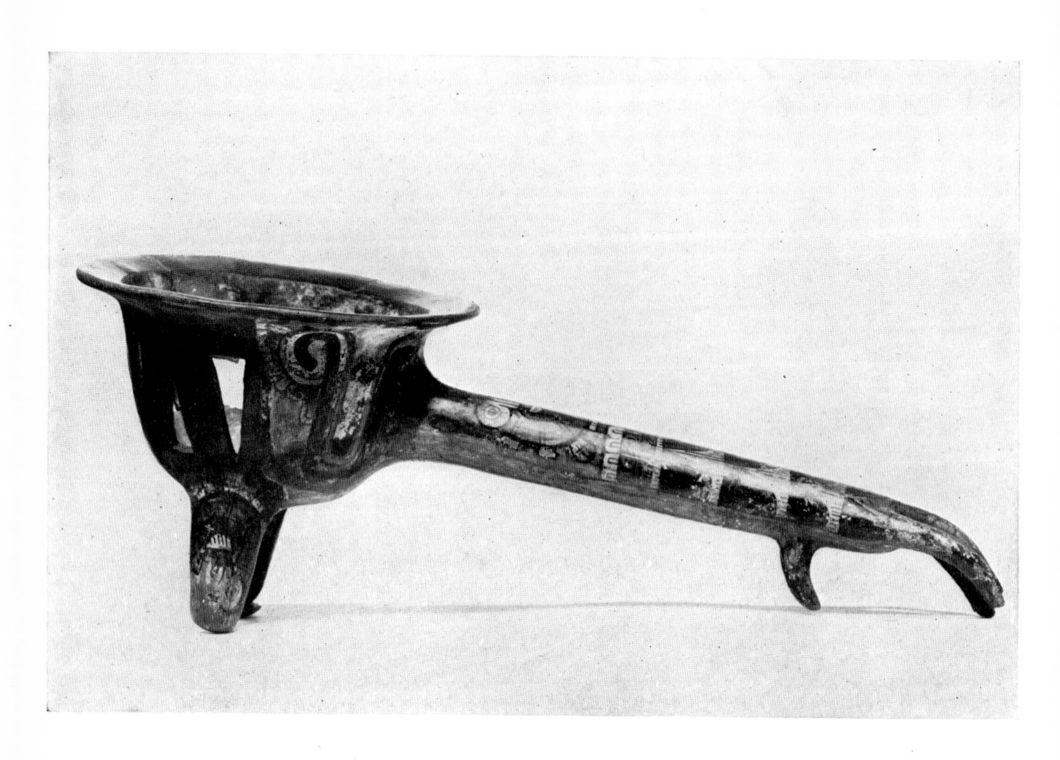

40. *Polychrome incense burner. Mixteca Puebla culture.*
Length 1 *ft.* $10\frac{3}{4}$ *in. British Museum*
(*See p.* 24).

41. *Pedestal bowl with yellow and black ornament on red. Aztec IV period, probably from Cholula or Tlascala. Ht.* 5$\frac{9}{10}$ *in. British Museum*

(*See p.* 25)

42. *Ovate vase with incised and red-painted ornament of centipedes on a yellow ground. From Otates, Vera Cruz Province. Ht.* $6\frac{5}{16}$ *in. Museo Nacional de Antropología, Mexico*

(*See p.* 25)

43A. *Chocolate pot with brown slip and incised ornament. Probably Totonac, from Isla de los Sacrificios. Ht.* $3\frac{3}{4}$ *in. British Museum.* (*See p.* 25)

43B. *Chocolate pot with black and white painted and relief ornament. Huaxtec. Ht.* $11\frac{1}{2}$ *in. British Museum.* (*See p.* 25)

44A. *Bowl with geometric black and white ornament on buff. Totonac, from Isla de los Sacrificios. Ht.* $4\frac{1}{10}$ *in. British Museum.* (*See p.* 25)

44B. *Bowl on anthropomorphic tripod supports, black and white ornament on buff. Totonac, from Isla de los Sacrificios. Diam.* $7\frac{4}{5}$ *in. British Museum.* (*See p.* 25)

45. *Pedestal vase with black and white ornament on orange. Totonac, from Isla de los Sacrificios. Ht.* $10\frac{1}{5}$ *in.*
British Museum
(*See p.* 25)

46A. *Biscuit-ware tripod vase with rattle pellets in the feet. Panama. Ht.* $5\frac{1}{8}$ *in. British Museum*
(*See p.* 26)

46B. *Biscuit-ware olla with armadillo heads in relief. Chiriqui, Panama. Ht.* $6\frac{2}{5}$ *in. British Museum*
(*See p.* 26)

47A. *Olla, lost colour ware. Panama. Ht.* $3\frac{1}{2}$ *in. British Museum*
(*See p.* 26)
47B. *Olla with alligator ornament. Panama.*
Ht. $3\frac{1}{2}$ *in. British Museum*
(*See p.* 26)

48. *Pyriform pedestal vase. Nicoya.*
Ht. 14$\frac{1}{10}$ *in. British Museum*
(*See p.* 27)

49A. *Polychrome bowl, Luna ware, Nicaragua.*
$9\frac{3}{10}$ *in. British Museum*
(*See p.* 27)

49B. *Tripod bowl with zoomorphic ornament in relief. Nicoya.*
Ht. $7\frac{1}{10}$ *in. British Museum*
(*See p.* 27)

50. *Cupisnique stirrup-spouted jar.*
Ht. $7\frac{5}{8}$ *in. British Museum*
(*See p.* 31)

51. *Cupisnique stirrup-spouted jar. Width* $6\frac{5}{8}$ *in.*
British Museum
(*See p.* 32)

52. *Recuay jar decorated with black negative painting over red and white. Ht.* $5\frac{3}{10}$ *in. British Museum*

(*See p.* 33)

53. *Mochica frog-jar with stirrup spout. Ht. 8 in.*
Cambridge University Museum of Archaeology and Ethnology
(*See p.* 34)

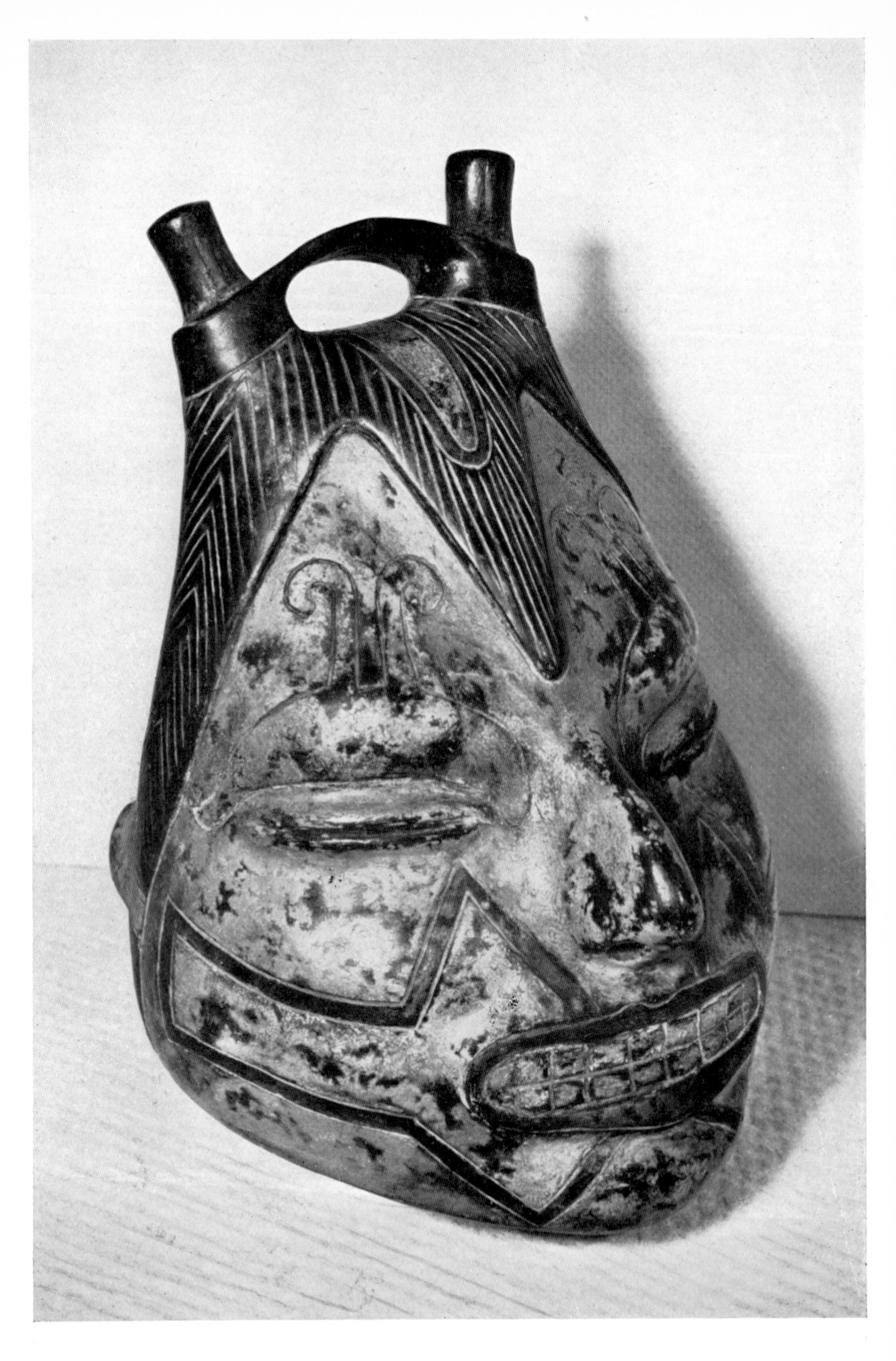

54. *Paracas Cavernas double-spouted polychrome jar representing deformed trophy head. Ht. 6$\frac{7}{8}$ in.*
Etnografiska Museet, Goteborg, Sweden
(*See p.* 33)

55. *Side view of Plate* 54

56. *Mochica stirrup-spouted jar with spiral ornament in low relief. Ht. $10\frac{2}{5}$ in. British Museum.* (*See pp.* 34, 35)

57. *Mochica jar, painted with scene showing messengers running. Ht. 11$\frac{7}{10}$ in. British Museum*
(See p. 35)

58. *Mochica dipper. Diam. 7 in.*
Cambridge University Museum of Archaeology and Ethnology
(*See p.* 34)

59. *Reverse of Plate* 58

60. *Modelled and painted Mochica jar showing shell-fish demons.*
Ht. 10$\frac{1}{10}$ *in. British Museum*
(*See p.* 35)

61. *Modelled and painted Mochica jar showing birds.*
Ht. 7$\frac{4}{5}$ *in. British Museum*
(*See p.* 35)

62. *Nazca polychrome vessels*

A. *Miniature trophy head. Ht.* $2\frac{1}{2}$ *in.*

B. *Miniature double-spouted jar with painted design of beans and trophy heads. Ht.* $3\frac{1}{4}$ *in.*

C. *Double-spouted jar with painted feline demon holding trophy heads. Ht.* 6 *in.*

All Cambridge University Museum of Archaeology and Ethnology. (*See p.* 35)

63. *Nazca Polychrome vessels*

A. *Miniature bowl with painted humming birds. Diam 4 in.*

B. *Effigy jar with many-headed demon painted on lower portion. Ht. 7½ in.*

Both Cambridge University Museum of Archaeology and Ethnology

(*See p.* 35)

64. *Tiahuanaco polychrome beaker (restored) showing painted puma. Ht. 6½ in.*
Cambridge University Museum of Archaeology and Ethnology
(*See p.* 36)

65. *Tiahuanaco polychrome bowl (restored) showing painted puma. Ht. 7 in.*
Cambridge University Museum of Archaeology and Ethnology
(*See p.* 36)

66. *Coast Tiahuanaco polychrome vessels*
A. *Cup with head design. Ht.* $3\frac{1}{2}$ *in.*
Cambridge University Museum of Archaeology and Ethnology. (*See p.* 37)
B. *Vase with double spout and bridge handle. Ht.* 6 *in.*
British Museum. (*See p.* 37)

67. *Chancay black-on-white figure jar. Ht. 17 in.*
Cambridge University Museum of Archaeology and Ethnology
(*See p.* 38)

68A. *Ica buff-ware bowl with textile-derived patterns in black, white and red. 4½ in.*
Cambridge University Museum of Archaeology and Ethnology. (*See p.* 38)
68B. *Chimu black-ware stirrup-spouted jar representing two fishermen on a 'balsa' raft made of bundles of reeds. Ht. 9½ in.*
Cambridge University Museum of Archaeology and Ethnology. (*See pp.* 38-9)

69. *Inca aryballus with black and white designs on red. Ht.* 13 *in.*
Cambridge University Museum of Archaeology and Ethnology
(*See p.* 39)

70A. *Provincial Inca bird-headed plate with black designs on white and red. From Chile. Diam.* $6\frac{1}{2}$ *in.*
Cambridge University Museum of Archaeology and Ethnology
(*See p.* 39)
70B. *Inca bowl with designs in black, white and red. Maximum diam.* $8\frac{3}{5}$ *in. British Museum*
(*See p.* 39)

71. *Inca 'paccha' or ceremonial drinking vessel, incorporating an aryballus and a model of a maize cob. Maximum ht.* $15\frac{1}{2}$ *in.*
British Museum
(*See p.* 39)

72A. *Dark-brown ware animal bowl. North Highlands of Ecuador.*
Diam. of opening, 4 in.
Cambridge University Museum of Archaeology and Ethnology. (*See p.* 41)

72B. *Bowl of Tuncahuan style, with monkeys and other designs in black negative painting, over red lines dividing the interior of the bowl; all on a buff slip. Province of Carchi, North Highlands of Ecuador.*
Diam. $8\frac{1}{2}$ *in.*
Cambridge University Museum of Archaeology and Ethnology. (*See p.* 41)

73. *Pottery from the Highlands of Ecuador*
A. *Polished red-ware bowl, shape possibly derived from a star-shaped stone club. Ht.* 4 *in.*
B. *Red-on-buff bowl, with monkeys in relief on the rim. Ht.* 4½ *in.*
Both Cambridge University Museum of Archaeology and Ethnology
(*See p.* 41)

74. *Jar decorated in thick white paint over a chocolate slip. Province of Cañar, Southern Highlands of Ecuador. Ht.* $17\frac{1}{2}$ *in. Cambridge University Museum of Archaeology and Ethnology*
(*See p.* 42)

75. Grey-ware jar with polished decoration. Santa Elena Peninsula, Province of Guayas, Coast of Ecuador. Ht. 17 in. Cambridge University Museum of Archaeology and Ethnology
(See p. 43)

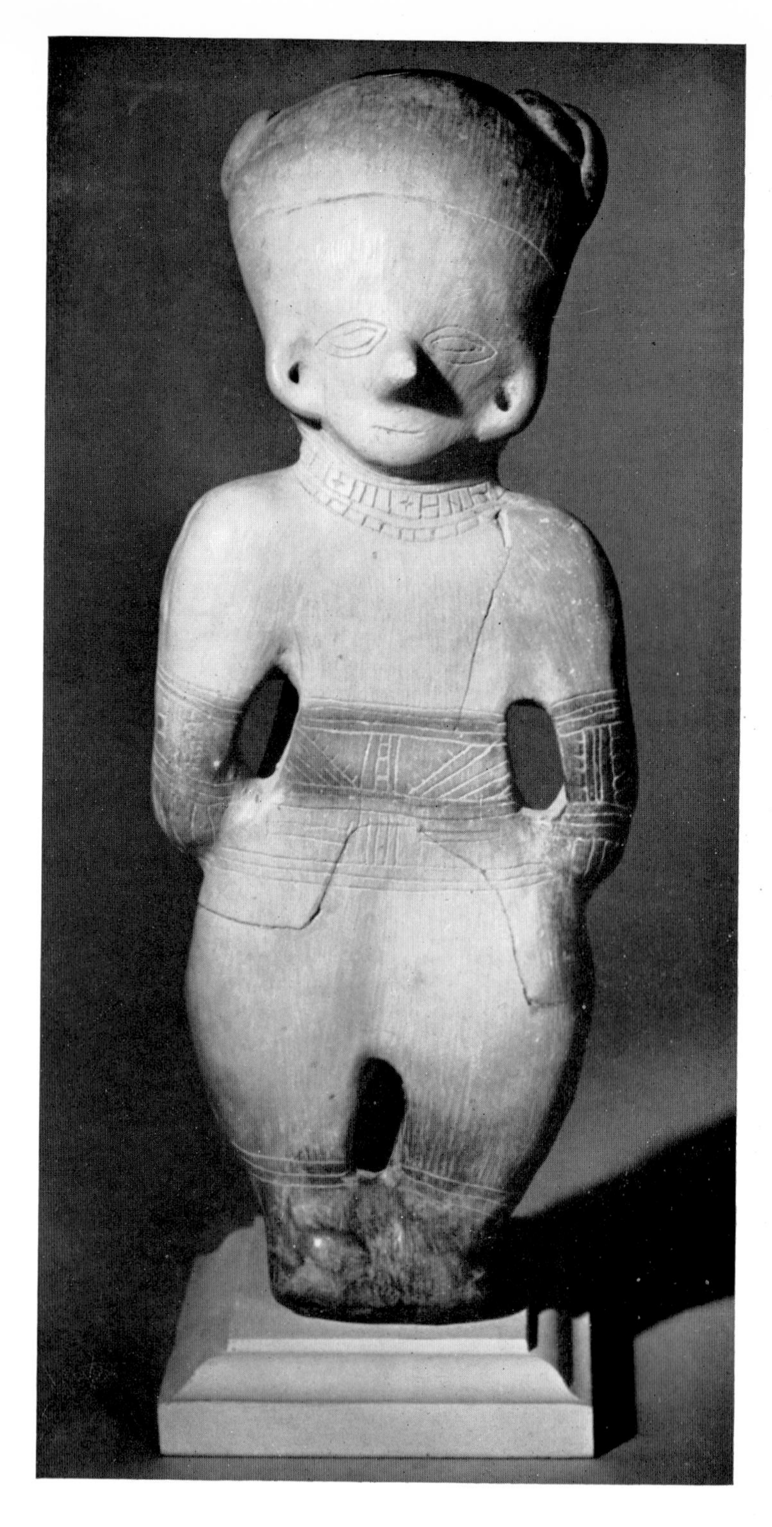

76. *Red whistle-figurine. Santa Elena Peninsula, Province of Guayas, Coast of Ecuador. Ht.* 11 *in.*
Cambridge University Museum of Archaeology and Ethnology
(*See p.* 42)

77. *Chibcha figurine. Province of Cundinamarca, Colombia. Ht. 8 in. Cambridge University Museum of Archaeology and Ethnology*
(*See p.* 43)

78. *Quimbaya jar, with black negative painting over white and red. Cauca Valley, Colombia. Ht. 10 in. Cambridge University Museum of Archaeology and Ethnology*
(*See p.* 44)

79A. *Chilean Diaguite duck pot, red, white and grey.*
North coast of Chile. Maximum ht. 5 in.
Cambridge University Museum of Archaeology and Ethnology. (*See p.* 45)
79B. *Quimbaya champlevé bowl of red-ware with vertically pierced lugs.*
Diam. of mouth 4 in.
Cambridge University Museum of Archaeology and Ethnology. (*See p.* 44)

80. *Belen urn, black on red. North-west Argentina. Ht.* 12 *in. Cambridge University Museum of Archaeology and Ethnology*
(*See pp.* 45-6)